INSIDE SECRETS OF
Finding a
Teaching Job

THIRD EDITION

The Most Effective Search Methods for Both New and Experienced Educators

Jack Warner and Clyde Bryan

with Diane Warner

jist *Works*
America's Career Publisher

Inside Secrets of Finding a Teaching Job, Third Edition

© 2006 by JIST Publishing, Inc.
Published JIST Works, an imprint of JIST Publishing, Inc.
8902 Otis Avenue
Indianapolis, IN 46216-1033
Phone: 1-800-648-JIST   Fax: 1-800-JIST-FAX   E-mail: info@jist.com

Visit our Web site at **www.jist.com** for information on JIST, free job search tips, book chapters, and ordering instructions for our many products! For free information on 14,000 job titles, visit **www.careeroink.com**.

Quantity discounts are available for JIST books. Have future editions of JIST books automatically delivered to you on publication through our convenient standing order program. Please call our Sales Department at 1-800-648-5478 for a free catalog and more information.

Trade Product Manager: Lori Cates Hand
Development and Copy Editor: Gayle Johnson
Interior Designer: Aleata Howard
Page Layout: Toi Davis
Cover Designer: Nick Anderson
Proofreader: Paula Lowell
Indexer: Tina Trettin

Printed in the United States of America
11 10 09 08 07 06   9 8 7 6 5 4 3 2 1

Library of Congress Cataloging-in-Publication Data

Warner, Jack, 1935-
    Inside secrets of finding a teaching job : the most effective search methods for both new and experienced educators / Jack Warner and Clyde Bryan with Diane Warner.-- 3rd ed.
        p. cm.
    Includes bibliographical references and index.
    ISBN-13: 978-1-59357-295-2 (alk. paper)
    ISBN-10: 1-59357-295-6 (alk. paper)
1. Teachers--Employment--United States. 2. Teaching--Vocational guidance--United States. 3. Employment interviewing--United States. 4. Job hunting--United States. I. Bryan, Clyde, 1935- II. Warner, Diane. III. Title.

LB1780.W37 2006
370'.2373--dc22
                                                        2006002407

ISBN-13: 978-1-59357-295-2
ISBN-10: 1-59357-295-6

Dedication

Dedicated to the memory of Beth Bryan.

You were always there for us. We love you.

Jack, Clyde, and Diane

Acknowledgments

We want to thank Lori Cates Hand, our editor, for her faith in us and for her encouragement and suggestions as we worked on this edition. We also want to thank all those who helped us with the research for this book, including the school administrators and members of interview panels who shared their inside secrets with us so that we could pass them on to you. Our appreciation and thanks also go to the hundreds of teacher candidates and new teachers who participated in our research survey and passed along their best words of advice.

We sincerely appreciate the help of Karlee Myers. A very special thanks to Holly Myers, who spent many hours helping us update and revise this edition. Thanks, Holly!

Special Thanks to the Professional Resume Writers Who Contributed to This Book

Laura DeCarlo	Rhoda Kopy	Ross Primack
Deborah Wile Dib	Rolande LaPointe	Igor Shpudejko
Dayna Feist	Andrea Peak	Kelley Smith
Susan Guarneri	Teresa L. Pearson	Linda Wunner

About This Book

A crisis has developed in the world of teaching: There is a dire shortage of teacher candidates in our country. According to a report released by the National Education Association (NEA), the United States has approximately 3 million classroom teachers. However, more than 2 million new teachers will be needed in the coming years, and not that many new teachers are graduating from teacher colleges. The teacher shortage has been caused by a number of factors:

- Many states have downsized their student-to-teacher ratios, which obviously requires more teachers.
- Many more immigrant children are entering school.
- Several parts of the country have booming populations where local colleges are not producing enough K–12 teachers.
- The current teaching force is aging, with a steady stream of retirees.
- Teachers are leaving the profession after only a few years in the field due to burnout and low pay.
- Many teachers in the fields of math, science, and computer technology have left the teaching profession for better-paying jobs in private industry. (This is why there is such a need in these fields.)

Even though teachers are in high demand, teacher candidates are still striving for the plum positions in their specific area of expertise, in the district of their choice, and in a school that meets their requirements for location, student profile, and commute distance from their homes. So, even though there are plenty of jobs, it's still important to know how to land the specific position of your choice, instead of being placed in the least-desirable area and school within the district.

Also, in spite of the teacher shortage, the job search process itself has continued to become more complicated with each passing year. When we first interviewed for teaching positions, for example, we weren't a bit worried about the job market. We merely blitzed our favorite school districts with resumes and then sat back and waited to be called. The interviews usually were rather predictable. They generally were conducted by the site administrator in the principal's office. The questions asked were fairly basic:

- "What is your philosophy of education?"
- "How would you deal with individual differences in your classroom?"
- "How do you handle discipline problems?"

Today, however, the job search process has become far more structured, formal, and intimidating, and the teacher candidate is faced with a dizzying array of buzzwords: *mock interviews, demonstration videos, teacher portfolios, school surveys, networking,* and *role-playing.* The rules have changed. Teacher candidates must learn to sell themselves—becoming their own Madison Avenue ad campaigns, so to speak. Suddenly, they find themselves in the roles of publicist, telemarketer, research guru, consummate Internet nerd, networker, critic, and makeover artist. It has become a very complicated process!

Our goal in this book is to simplify the process for you by explaining every step, from the application to the interview. Best of all, we have included hundreds of fresh, relevant bits of advice gleaned from interviews conducted across the country.

First, we interviewed hundreds of teacher candidates who are currently in the job market, as well as those who have recently survived the job search process and landed a position. We asked them every question we could think of that might help you in your search, including what surprised them most about their interviews, what they wish they had known, and their best advice for those beginning the job search process.

We also picked the brains of administrators, teachers, personnel directors, department chairs, parents, specialists, instructional coordinators, mentor teachers, and others who sit on teacher interview panels. We asked them 16 basic questions, including these:

- What impresses you most about a resume or application?
- What do you learn from a candidate's body language?
- What questions should an interviewee ask and *not* ask during the interview?
- What turns you off in an interview?
- What is your best advice for teacher candidates today?

Talk about "inside secrets"—did we ever uncover them!

So sit back, relax, and get the real inside scoop!

Contents

Part 1

FINDING AND APPLYING FOR TEACHING JOBS

CHAPTER 1

Increasing Your Marketability

Finding the right teaching job takes a lot more than just sending out resumes. These days, looking for a job means creating and executing a complete self-marketing campaign.

The first step in marketing yourself is to *know yourself!* You've probably heard the expression in the world of retail sales, "know your product." In your case, your product is *you,* and you can't sell yourself unless you know your strengths and weaknesses.

After you've determined where you shine, you can create the components of your marketing campaign, including your mission statement, demonstration video, and teacher portfolio. In this chapter you will learn the basics of creating these marketing tools, as well as ways you can make yourself more marketable. In chapter 3, we discuss other tools in your marketing campaign—including your resume and cover letters.

Assess Your Strengths and Weaknesses

If you've just graduated from college, you've probably been so consumed by your hectic academic schedule that you haven't given this subject of your strengths and weaknesses much thought. But now is the time, and it's imperative that you do so. Why is it so important? Because being aware of your personal strengths and weaknesses is a prerequisite to the other steps you must take to market yourself as the top-notch classroom teacher you know you can be. For example, how can you prepare your mission statement, your resume, or your teacher portfolio if you don't *really* know yourself? Another important reason is this: You'll almost

> Virtually all of the teacher candidates and newly hired teachers in our survey said they were asked about their strengths and weaknesses in one way or another during their teacher interviews.

certainly be asked to tell about your strengths and weaknesses during your teacher interviews.

From our survey of teacher applicants all over the United States, we found several questions you can count on being asked at the interview table. These are covered in chapter 6. But you should know this from the start: The one that is *virtually always asked* deals with your strengths and weaknesses. More than likely, it will be put to you in the form of a command rather than a question: "Tell me about your strengths and weaknesses." Think about this for a minute: What is the interviewer *really* asking?

What the interviewer really wants to know is this: "Why should we hire you? What can you do for our students? Why should we choose you over the rest of the candidates we're interviewing today?"

So when you're asked about your strengths and weaknesses, you should consider it an open-ended question, a golden opportunity to *sell* yourself—or, as we hear so often these days, a chance to be your own publicist. You need to tout your strengths and minimize any weakness by presenting it as a strength. This is actually quite easy to do, as you will see.

Your Strengths

You have many specific skills and positive character traits. Some are tangible; others are intangible.

Your tangible skills include those that are related to the teaching profession in general—including your ability to teach on the elementary or secondary level—and specific skills, such as your ability to work with bilingual or gifted children. You will list most of these job-related skills on your application and resume, so the interview panel will already be familiar with them. However, you might have many other tangible skills that are not shown on your resume but that will greatly enhance your chances of being hired.

For example, you might have coached Little League, taught swimming lessons, or been a camp counselor. Or perhaps you worked your way through college by tutoring struggling students. These all require skills that are transferable to the classroom. Your hobbies often involve transferable skills as well. For example, you might enjoy working with puppets, playing the guitar, surfing the Net, playing chess, sewing, or crafting.

By the way, if you're having trouble identifying your skills, the next time you're at the library, check out a copy of *What Color Is Your Parachute?* by Richard Bolles. This book will help you uncover your hidden skills and talents. By the time you're through discovering your skills, you'll be oozing with self-confidence.

Next we come to your intangible skills. These could also be called "invisible" skills, because they have to do with your personality, your character, and your ability to get along with others. Are you patient? Caring? Trustworthy? Loyal? Responsible? Self-disciplined? Honest? Positive? Do you have a sense of humor? Do you get along well with others? Do you have a strong work ethic? Do you really *love* young people? Are you *excited* about becoming a teacher? Are you a dependable, punctual person? Do you enjoy working on a team? Do you get a charge out of motivating students? If so, let the interview panel know. They may never know unless you tell them!

And how about your leadership qualities? Are you a good organizer? Then *tell* the interviewer so! And be prepared to illustrate your skills with *specific* examples. For example, tell about the time you worked with a group of parents to coordinate a fund-raiser, or how you initiated a neighborhood-watch program in your subdivision.

Remember, the interview panel is looking for reasons to hire you, reasons why you're the one they want on their staff. So give them all the information they need to make the right choice.

> "Be prepared to give the answer that wants to be heard."
> —ESL/English teacher in Vancouver, British Columbia

Why are these intangible qualities so important? Because the interview committee already *knows* your academic background, including your college major and minor, what credentials you hold, and what you're qualified to teach. You wouldn't have been called for an interview in the first place if you didn't fit their needs in a professional sense. What they really want to know about—and what they can find out only during an interview—are your intangible strengths: those positive qualities that say you're an enthusiastic, likable, dependable person.

Be prepared to give specific examples of your strengths if asked. It's also a good idea to put one at the very top of your list, just in case you're asked, "What is your greatest strength?" Unless you've thought about it ahead of time and rehearsed your response, you might be caught off guard.

If you tell the panel that your greatest strength is your dependability, for example, be prepared to explain how you're always the first one in the parking lot in the morning because you don't like to be late for work. If your greatest strength is that you relate well to kids, tell them how much fun you had teaching swimming lessons last summer and how well you got along with the children and their parents.

A word of caution: Don't get *too* carried away with the details; make your case and move on. In 30 seconds to a minute you can, with practice, build a very strong case for yourself when asked about your greatest strength. Don't beat it to death!

"You have about 30 minutes to sell yourself to the interview committee, to make them want to hire you. This is your one and only chance, so be prepared!"
—Elementary school principal in St. Louis, Missouri

Your Weaknesses

After you've told the panel about your strengths, expect to be asked about your weaknesses. Fortunately, your weaknesses or "limitations" don't have to work against you at the interview table. You know your limitations, but don't be too quick to plead guilty to a weakness if you can turn it around and convert it into something that will make you look good.

When you're faced with the question "Tell us about your weaknesses," don't get negative and immediately begin to explain how you don't like to teach science because it's always been difficult for you, or that you never quite had the interest in it that you have in other areas, blah, blah, blah. Right away you've turned off the committee and told them just about all they want to hear on the subject.

The fact that multi-subject teachers feel more prepared to teach some subject areas than others is a given, so try to stay away from specific academic subject areas or job-related classroom skills. Instead, talk about your most "angelic" weakness—one that can be turned into a positive. Here are some examples:

Don't say:

> *"I'm a poor manager of my time."*

Do say:

> *"Sometimes I have so many good ideas and things I want to accomplish with the kids that I get frustrated when I run out of time."*

Don't say:

> *"I'm such a nitpicker that it gets in the way of my progress."*

Do say:

> *"I'm too demanding of myself—too much of a perfectionist."*

Don't say:

> *"I never seem to be able to reach my goals."*

6

Do say:

> *"My expectations for myself and my students are high, and with time constraints I feel I don't always reach my goals."*

Don't say:

> *"I have very little patience with people who waste my time."*

Do say:

> *"When working or planning with others, I sometimes get frustrated when the time is not used efficiently—going down too many rabbit trails. I have had to teach myself to be patient."*

Whatever you do, don't confess to a weakness in classroom management or in a certain subject area. You'll only be digging a hole for yourself! Instead, take one of your most "innocent" and "harmless" weaknesses and turn it into a positive.

Prepare a Mission Statement

Now that you've assessed your strengths and weaknesses, you're in a perfect frame of mind to work on your mission statement. So what is a mission statement, and why do you need one?

Professionally speaking, a mission statement is what has been called your "philosophy of education," "career statement," or "vision statement." It seems that everyone has a mission statement these days: Corporations, associations, organizations, individuals, and families all proudly display them. These mission statements usually include an all-encompassing purpose and vision for the person's or family's life, the association's policies and goals, or the corporation's philosophy of doing business, interacting with its employees, serving the public, and so on.

> "The only limit to the realization of tomorrow will be our doubts of today."
> —Franklin Delano Roosevelt

A teacher's mission statement pertains specifically to the teaching profession. If you take it seriously and write it thoughtfully, it can be one of the most powerful and significant things you ever compose. It will become a compass to guide you for the rest of your professional life.

A mission statement typically includes some or all of these components:

- **Who you are:** Your strengths, skills, talents, and personality traits
- **Your guiding principles:** Your beliefs, standards, and character traits
- **Your passion for teaching:** Why you are passionate about teaching, and how your strengths and beliefs will benefit your students and career

- **Your vision as a teacher:** Where you plan to be professionally five or ten years from now, including your goals for professional growth, future credentials, or certificates
- **Your legacy:** How you hope to make a difference by positively affecting the lives of students and peers

One Teacher's Mission Statement

Here is an example of a teacher's mission statement:

My mission is:

"To dedicate my life to the teaching profession, always nurturing and encouraging my students.

To create a classroom with a challenging environment so that every student will reach his or her maximum potential intellectually and socially.

To use my creative skills, particularly in the fields of art and music, to enhance and inspire the lives of my students.

To share my optimism and generally sunny disposition with everyone I meet, especially my students, their parents, and my peers.

To continue to grow as a teacher and as a person, taking advantage of professional classes and seminars, eventually earning my administrative credential.

To value my students, to show them respect, and to build their self-esteem in some way every day. When my students are my age, I want to be the teacher who stands out in their memories because they knew I cared."

What Details Should My Mission Statement Include?

The preceding mission statement is quite powerful. Your statement may be longer or shorter. Here are examples of details you might consider including:

- An experience or person who motivated you to go into education
- What you specifically hope to accomplish within your discipline
- Why you value the American family, including your own, and how you plan to incorporate these values into your teaching
- Your philosophies of teaching children and managing your classroom
- How you plan to deal with your students' individual differences
- Rewarding student-teaching experiences you had that you hope to repeat with your own class of students

- Your belief that *every* child, regardless of socioeconomic or ethnic background, deserves the same quality of instruction and challenging learning experiences
- Your belief that a teacher should be a role model
- Why every student should be given the opportunity to utilize technology
- Why each student should be challenged to develop critical-thinking skills and become a lifelong learner
- Your belief that students should be stimulated and motivated so that they'll want to stay in school
- Why students should be treasured, respected, nurtured, praised, and encouraged
- Your desire to be a team player, willing to contribute to the extra activities of the school and the community
- Why your students should be taught a sense of responsibility for themselves, each other, and for the Earth's resources

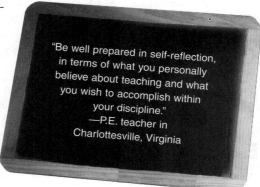

"Be well prepared in self-reflection, in terms of what you personally believe about teaching and what you wish to accomplish within your discipline."
—P.E. teacher in Charlottesville, Virginia

- Your desire to find a school and staff that nurture a rich multicultural environment for learning
- Why students should be guided firmly, but with kindness and fairness
- Your high expectations for your students—and your patience to help them reach those expectations
- Your desire to develop the whole person so that your students will be prepared not only for college but to enter the workforce and have families of their own
- Your goal to have each of your high school seniors graduate with the ability to live a productive life, to love himself and others, and to continue to have a love of learning

These are just a few examples to get your creative juices flowing. What do you truly believe? What drives you to become a teacher? Only you know where your passions lie, which is why

"A teacher affects eternity; no one can tell where his influence stops."
—Henry Adams

every mission statement is different. There's no set formula, and we can't dictate what you should say.

Benefits of Having a Mission Statement

Whether your mission statement is long or short, you'll find it an invaluable tool for several important reasons:

- It clarifies things in your mind: your strengths, your passions, your goals, and your future.
- It helps you see exactly where you've come from, where you are now, and where you're headed in the years to come. Although you might not realize it, your mission statement will be a tremendous help as you sell yourself in the job market. For example, it will give you direction as you write your resume and cover letter, create your teacher portfolio, conduct your school surveys, do your networking, and interact during your job interviews.
- Maybe best of all, you'll be ready when they ask the inevitable question during the interview: "Tell us about yourself."

Extras Count

It's safe to say that you should include anything extra you can add to your resume and portfolio to increase your marketability: your talents, experiences, skills, and positive character traits. The idea, of course, is to make yourself stand out from the rest.

Let's assume that in marketing your product, you've included all these things, and you have a great resume (chapter 3 covers resume writing). Let's also assume you had a very encouraging, successful student teaching experience, and you've even gained valuable teaching experience through substitute teaching. These are all pluses, but many other applicants might offer essentially the same package.

Yes! I'll Pursue That Extra Credential or Certificate!

Everything else being equal, it might be the teacher with the extra certificate or credential who lands the job. We understand, having been down that road ourselves a few times, that an extra credential or certificate is not easy to come by. It requires more time, more work, and more money. And maybe it's impossible for you to pursue one at this time. What we've learned, however, not only from teachers currently in the job market but also from those who sit on interview panels, is that having a second credential or certificate makes a candidate more attractive to the school district.

A credential or certificate in one of these three areas can greatly enhance your chances of getting a job:

- **Bilingual education certificate of competence** (depending, of course, on the number of limited-English-proficient or language-minority students in the district and how committed the district is to bilingual education)
- **Speech/language credential**
- **Special-education credential**

The availability of jobs in these areas often far exceeds the supply of credentialed candidates. And many of the teacher applicants we talked with said interview panels asked them whether they would be willing to pursue an extra credential or certificate if hired; 43 percent of these applicants said they would.

> In our survey, 3 percent of the teacher candidates considered themselves bilingual, and 9 percent had some type of special-education credential.

If you're still in college and your long-range goal is to work in speech therapy, special education, bilingual education, or some other specialty, you might want to pursue the extra credential now, in conjunction with your teaching credential. That way, you'll have a leg up on your competition, making yourself more attractive during the hiring process.

However, if you've completed your credential work and you don't already have an extra credential or certificate, we recommend that you agree to pursue one if you're asked to. This question might come up at the interview table. If you go into the interview with a ready, positive response, this will put you in better stead than those who hesitate at the idea.

One last comment on this subject: If you're looking for a position in a state or district with a heavy concentration of language-minority students, you might soon find that the extra certificate in bilingual education is almost mandatory. And if you're in one of the increasing number of states with a strong commitment to bilingual education, you would also do well to pursue this as a second certificate.

> According to the National Center for Education Statistics, the percentage of children ages 5 to 17 who speak a language other than English at home grew from 3.8 million in 1979 to 9.9 million in 2003. This means that 19 percent of students speak a language other than English.

Here are some other excellent areas to consider for an additional credential or certificate:

- Vocational education
- Computer education
- English as a second language (ESL)
- Library science (or educational media)
- Counseling and guidance
- Administration (after you have some teaching experience)

Whether you're a multiple-subject or single-subject teacher, you should consider adding that extra certificate or credential in an area that interests you.

Yes! I'll Teach Any Grade Level!

Another extra that can make you more attractive to a school district is to be flexible about which grade level or subject area you will teach. If you're willing to teach any of three or four grades or subjects, for example, you're much more useful to the district, and this significantly improves your marketability. You could mention this flexibility in your cover letter. Also be prepared to respond favorably to the idea during the interview.

Your willingness to be flexible increases your marketability in another important way: As you've already seen, interview committees often ask questions that have more than one purpose. If they ask whether you're willing to teach grade levels other than the one for which you are interviewing, it might be because they've filled that particular position—but they have another.

They might also be trying to determine how flexible you are. You see, school districts are looking for teachers who are team players and who have great attitudes. They might not actually need you to teach at another grade level at all. They might simply be testing you to see whether you're willing to fit in with *their* plans and meet *the district's* needs as they change from year to year.

Good administrators do not hire for the here and now; they hire for the long haul. Perhaps a community is growing because a new company is relocating there, creating 3,000 job openings. A good school administrator looks at that community and sees the need for many new teachers. On the other hand, perhaps a company with 500 employees plans to move elsewhere in two years. A wise administrator wants teachers on board who can teach multiple grades or more than one subject because the school's enrollment is likely to decline. Birth rates also come into play. Although the number of children born annually might be static in any given community, there will always be occasional peaks and valleys in the birth rate. As large or small classes work their way through the school system, administrators need personnel who are *flexible*.

If you can convince an interview panel that you're enthusiastic about teaching a variety of age groups within their school or district, they can see the following: "This candidate has the same qualifications as the others we've interviewed today, but this one is willing to fit in where we can use him best. This kind of flexible attitude is exactly what we're looking for."

> In our survey, 71 percent of the teacher candidates were willing to accept positions at any grade level or in any subject for which they were qualified.

Look at it this way: Most teacher credential programs require student teachers to teach at two different grade levels anyway, so you've undoubtedly had the experience, and the interview committee knows this. But whether you're interviewing for a position at the elementary, middle school, or secondary level, the very fact that you don't balk at the possibility of teaching several grade levels up or down from your ideal will impress them.

If you're *determined* to hold out for a fifth- or sixth-grade position, or if your heart is set on teaching *only* honors English to bright high school seniors, maybe you should consider the interviewers' perspective for a moment. They might respect your desire to hold to your ideals. Or the next interviewee in the door might get the job instead of you because of his or her flexibility (sometimes interpreted as *attitude*).

This might seem like a small thing, but if you really want to stand out from the rest and increase your chances of being hired, give this idea some serious thought.

Yes! I'll Teach at Any School!

If you're interviewing in a *great* district where you would *love* to teach at *any* school, and you're offered a position that fits in with your goals and vision for your future in education, it's a no-brainer: *Sign the contract,* regardless of school placement.

But what if you're interviewing with a district where only one or two schools are attractive to you—and you're not crazy about the idea of teaching at any of the others? If you're offered a position in this district and they ask whether you'd be willing to teach at *any* school, what should you do?

Before you answer that question, remember that they *might* be checking out your flexibility and your willingness to fit in where their needs dictate. If you're willing to go to any school, you become much more valuable than another candidate who's holding out for only one or two schools. *Don't knock yourself out of the running because of a lack of flexibility.*

If you're sincere in your job search—if you really need a job—you must be willing to accept a first-year position at any school within a district. Then, in a year or two, if you still prefer another campus and a position opens up, you can apply for a lateral transfer. If you've done a good job, chances are you'll be given preference over someone new to the district.

If you're determined to hold out for a certain school in the district, you might be passing up a chance to be hired. You see—and this is one of our "inside secrets"—other tenured teachers within the district might be applying for a lateral transfer to that position as well, which means you're competing against one of their own. But, you say, this leaves another vacancy open, doesn't it? Exactly! But you won't be considered for it unless you agree *at the time of the interview* to accept any vacancy that opens up.

Look at this as a game of musical chairs. When the music stops, someone is left without a chair. Kind of a sinking feeling. Embarrassing, too. But your job search is not a game. This is your career. And although we believe you should *not* accept a position in September that you'll wish you could leave in November, we also believe you shouldn't be *too* selective. (The key word is *too*.)

Of course you should try for the plum, that ideal job that is at the top of your wish list. But there comes a time when good judgment and conventional wisdom dictate taking a position if offered and then looking at making a change or applying for a transfer a few years down the road.

We talked with many teacher candidates who said that their interviews went extremely well, but they were never offered a position, and they didn't know why. It could be that they were holding out for a certain school, and their inflexibility killed their chances of being hired.

Put Your Heart into It

If you do accept a position at a school other than the one you wanted, here's one word of caution: Be sure you put your heart and soul into it, as you'll be expected to do. In fact, throughout your first year, give yourself an attitude check occasionally to be sure you're not just "riding this one out" until something better comes along. More than likely, you'll find that you're working with a good group of colleagues, and you might just discover that you're really happy right where you are. As we look back over our careers, we find that some of our most rewarding experiences came from the most difficult, challenging situations. Adversity sometimes brings out the best in us.

> Fifty percent of the teacher candidates in our survey pursued every job opportunity, even though the positions weren't exactly what they wanted.

On the other hand, if after a year or two at the first school you decide to apply for a transfer within the district, at least you'll have established yourself and probably received your tenure. Also, you'll be much more knowledgeable about the schools in the district and where you might like to go next. There's definitely stress involved in making a move of any kind, but if you think you would be happier at a different school, the stress might be worth it.

Just remember that in education, as in every other profession, you don't always start out exactly where you think you want to be. Lateral moves can come later. You could call that playing the "seniority card," but it's often the road you must take to get to your ideal position and school. A word of caution: You also need to be fair to yourself. Don't sign a contract for a situation so bad that you would pay to get out of it a month later.

Other Options: Private Schools and Schools in Other Cities and States

While we're on the subject of being flexible about where you'll teach, there are a couple more options to consider, neither of which should be considered second-best or only a place to start your career.

Private Schools

If there are private schools in your area, do some calling and include them when you conduct your school surveys (see chapter 2). You'll discover many types of private schools, including military academies, church or religious schools, daycare centers, nonsectarian independent schools, and college-preparatory boarding schools.

Some of these require their teachers to have state teaching credentials, and some do not. Also, church schools and those affiliated with religious denominations might expect their teachers to agree with their religious beliefs. A teacher's commitment to these beliefs might even be included in the teaching contract.

Private schools typically are unique in several ways, and there are advantages as well as disadvantages to teaching in one of them. One of the advantages is that they usually boast a smaller student-to-teacher ratio. Many teachers find themselves more suited to a private-school setting, especially if they agree with the school's theology or philosophy. Furthermore, you often find a close-knit camaraderie among the students, staff, and parents at private schools that a public school might not have.

The most obvious downside is often salary, because private schools usually aren't as well-funded as public schools. This factor alone keeps many teachers from considering a private school, even though they might otherwise enjoy the private-school experience. If the idea of teaching at one of these schools sounds attractive to you, check it out.

Private-school teaching vacancies might be listed with your college placement office or in the classified section of your local newspaper. The best sources, however, are the schools themselves; contact each one to request information and applications. If you know someone who teaches at a private school (or parents whose children attend one), talk with them to get a feel for the school and its policies.

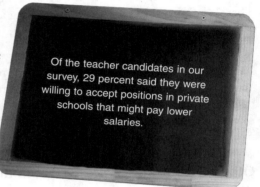

Of the teacher candidates in our survey, 29 percent said they were willing to accept positions in private schools that might pay lower salaries.

Teaching Outside Your Hometown

In our survey, we found that most candidates look for teaching positions close to their colleges or where they grew up. Although some candidates do find jobs in one of these two general areas, we suggest that you expand your job search area for these reasons:

- Typically, college towns have an oversupply of teacher candidates.
- Unless you're a "fourth-generation, been-here-forever, expect-to-be-here-forever" kind of person, you exclude some great opportunities by limiting your job search.

If you're willing to broaden your search area, a whole world of teaching opportunities is waiting for you. You can apply for vacancies not only in other districts throughout your home state, but in other states as well. Also, thousands of overseas teaching opportunities exist, such as teaching for a private American school abroad, for a major U.S. corporation, or for the military. The Department of Defense, for example, operates 210 schools with a total enrollment of more than 100,000 American students.

Overseas positions almost always require that you be credentialed in one of the 50 states and that you've done some graduate work or possess a graduate degree. Some also require fluency in a specific foreign language. Preference often is given to unmarried teachers or to teaching couples with no children because of the limited availability of housing.

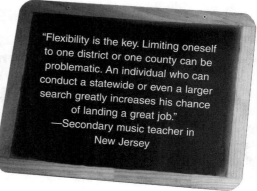

"Flexibility is the key. Limiting oneself to one district or one county can be problematic. An individual who can conduct a statewide or even a larger search greatly increases his chance of landing a great job."
—Secondary music teacher in New Jersey

If you're willing to consider teaching vacancies in other states, see the list of state departments of education and state offices of teacher credentialing in the appendix. It also lists some great resources for overseas employment.

Yes! I'll Consider a Half-Day Teaching Position!

Job-sharing is an idea that is catching on around the country. Here is the concept: Two teachers share a classroom, splitting the teaching hours evenly between them. For example, in a school district in Arizona, two teachers came to this job-sharing arrangement: One teaches in the morning and the other in the afternoon, with alternating full days on Fridays.

If the morning or afternoon teacher gives up her position, this obviously creates a half-day vacancy, which you may be willing to consider. In any case, accepting a half-day position is one way to get your foot in the door.

Make a Demonstration Video

Although school districts rarely require demonstration videos as part of the screening process, they are requested once in a while. Because of this, many colleges and universities have students make a demonstration video as part of their teacher-preparation courses. And a demo video is a necessity for anyone applying for a teaching position overseas or out of state, for which the interview might be conducted by telephone. In this case, the demo video gives you a leg up on your competition because the hiring panel can see you and has a better sense of your personality and teaching style.

As we researched this book, we found that 14 percent of those interviewed had prepared demonstration videos. Several reported having been asked by interview committees to leave a copy of their video for further review. Although such a request is not commonplace, it does happen—usually when the hiring panel is impressed with your performance at the interview and wants to see how you interact with a classroom full of students.

Showcase Your Best Performance

If you decide to put together a demo video, there are some things you should consider. The first is this: Play to your strengths. You know what you do best, so use that in your video. It might be a particular science lesson you taught during your student teaching or a group activity in which you assume the role of facilitator. If you're doing your student teaching, your master teacher will probably be glad to work with you on this and maybe even do the taping for you. Most schools have a video camera available, so all you need is a high-quality tape.

You'll find that things you enjoy the most are ordinarily the ones you do best, so plan on having your favorite lessons recorded on your demo video. Here are some ideas to consider:

- Teach a lesson to the entire class, including all the steps of a well-planned lesson.
- Teach a lesson to a smaller group.
- Interact with a small group of students in cooperative groups or at an interest center.
- Involve yourself in a physical-education or game type of activity.
- Direct a drama or musical event.
- Work with another teacher in a team situation.
- Work with the class or a small group on an art project.
- Teach a song or musical activity.
- Use manipulatives, especially as part of a science or math lesson.
- Work with students in a community-service setting.

Your video should include segments of more than one lesson. Each segment should be long enough to get your message across, but not so long that it becomes boring.

Remember that you're in complete control of what a hiring panel will see, so give them your best by demonstrating all the energy,

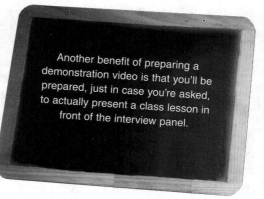

Another benefit of preparing a demonstration video is that you'll be prepared, just in case you're asked, to actually present a class lesson in front of the interview panel.

enthusiasm, and passion you can muster. Then use your demonstration video as one more way to sell yourself.

Distributing Your Video

Once you've completed your video, have copies made from the master. If you're lucky, you can make copies of your master at your college media center. Otherwise, look in the Yellow Pages under "Video Editing," "Video Production Services," or "Video Tape Duplication and Transfer Services."

When you have your copies, label them in a clear, professional way, and then put them to work for you. Let every school district know that you have a demonstration video available by mentioning this in your cover letter, and always have one with you during an interview. Offer it to the committee, even if they don't ask for it. If you've gone to the trouble and taken the time to create a video that showcases your talents, you should use it to your best advantage. It may be the "extra" that lands you the job.

Create a Teacher Portfolio

In the time since we wrote the first edition of this book, teacher portfolios have become hugely popular with hiring panels. In fact, most colleges and universities now require their students to create portfolios as part of their teacher-credential programs. As this trend continues, it won't be long before these portfolios become mandatory at the interview table.

What Is the Purpose of a Portfolio?

Before you begin filling your portfolio with everything in sight, consider its purpose. You can take a lesson from corporate America, where portfolios have been around for a long time; in fact, they've been the professional's preferred mode of "show and tell" for years. It's a given, for example, that commercial artists bring along their portfolios when they interview with Madison Avenue ad agencies. Their portfolios contain carefully chosen samples of their work that speak for them at the interview table and demonstrate their talents. They know they have one chance, and one chance only, to shine—to make a great impression. This is no time to be humble.

The same principle applies to teachers: Your portfolio should show off your very best work. Gather anything that demonstrates your talents, abilities, and accomplishments—anything that will put you in a special light with the hiring panel.

If you recently completed your student teaching, you probably have samples of your work, such as projects that took hours to prepare. If you haven't yet done your student teaching, however, begin thinking about your portfolio as you start your assignment.

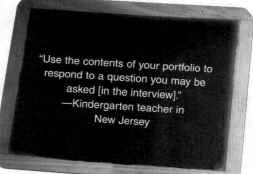

"Portfolios are nice, and here is a suggestion I found helpful: In the portfolio packets I assembled, I included a Recent Achievements page—sort of a summary of things I have done. This also helped me summarize my most recent accomplishments and have them handy and fresh in my mind."
—Second-grade teacher in a parochial school in Massachusetts

Your portfolio begins with a sturdy folder, an accordion-style filing jacket, a presentation binder, or a heavy-duty portfolio with pockets (see your local office-supply store for ideas). If you can afford it, you might even splurge on a leather-like portfolio, which has a professional look.

What to Include in Your Portfolio

You can fill your portfolio with anything you like—there are no rules. This section mentions some things you might want to include. Remember, the idea is to impress the interview panel with your accomplishments and talents as a teacher and to provide evidence of your transferable skills.

"Use the contents of your portfolio to respond to a question you may be asked [in the interview]."
—Kindergarten teacher in New Jersey

The basic general contents of your portfolio can include the following:

- Recent achievements page (a summary of what you've done lately)
- Resume
- Mission statement
- Professional letters of reference
- Letters from parents commending you for your work with their children
- Outstanding evaluations written by your university student-teaching supervisor or your master teacher
- Copies of teaching certificates and certificates of participation in workshops or seminars
- Examples of the ways you recognize students' achievements (Student of the Month awards and so on)

Specific classroom-related items to consider include the following:

- Photos of you presenting a lesson to a class or working with a small group of students
- Photos of special activities (such as you taking your students on a field trip, directing a drama or musical presentation, or participating as a school coach or yearbook advisor)
- Hands-on materials or manipulatives that you have incorporated into a lesson

Note: Hands-on activities and manipulatives are hot trends in education, so it's important for you to work them into the interview somehow, especially if you've used them in math or science. This holds true for both elementary and secondary educators.

- Samples of your students' work (artwork, creative writing, and so on)
- A copy of your demo video showing you in action (teaching a lesson, a song, or a game; working with a group of students or one-on-one with a student)
- Copies of a specific, well-designed lesson plan

You can also demonstrate your well-roundedness by including community-related items:

- Photos of you coaching a Little League team or working with children in the community in some way
- Photos of you working as a camp counselor, Sunday school teacher, or game director during a summer program
- Newspaper articles or photos that show you as a leader, team player, organizer, or role model

Note: Try to include photos that are happy and upbeat; you want to convince the interview panel that you love kids, you love to teach, and you're having a lot of fun! In a word—*smile!*

Presentation Hints

We suggest that you mount everything possible in photo matting with dark, clear captions at the top of each mounting. For example:

"Teaching a Math Lesson Using Manipulatives"

and

"Serving as a Summer Camp Counselor"

It's a good idea, by the way, to have an inexpensive duplicate of your portfolio on hand, just in case the interview panel asks you to leave one with them.

We hope we've sold you on the concept of a teacher portfolio. Creating one is simple enough, and a well-organized portfolio is one more tool to make you stand out. Even if the interview speeds by and you never have a chance to share anything from your portfolio, at least you will have scored "style points." We know this is true because so many of the administrators we interviewed said they were impressed when a teacher candidate brought a portfolio to the interview. It shows them you have that something extra—something your competition might not have.

> "Bring something to the interview, whether requested or not: a portfolio with photos of previous classroom time, a favorite lesson you designed or adapted, samples of your lessons or projects. This shows that you are prepared, even if the opportunity does not arise to show it. I've always noted when candidates have something with them when they come in. Just this alone tells me they want to further present what they can do. Attitude and interest matter a lot to me!"
>
> —Principal of a middle school in rural Virginia

Tip: If you *really* want to stand head and shoulders above other teacher candidates, make your portfolio available online as a *digital portfolio* presented on your own Web site. In addition to your resume, scan the contents of your portfolio, and include them in your digital portfolio. Any photographs that show you teaching a class or working with children in other ways can be in a digital format if they are taken with a digital camera or scanned and saved as graphics files. You can then post these photos in your online portfolio. By the way, be sure that your resume includes a reference to your digital portfolio, such as the following: "Portfolio available for viewing on my Web site: www.HenryJames.com."

You might want to limit your digital portfolio to the best of your physical portfolio. Anyone scanning your portfolio online might not have the time or patience to go through everything, especially your digital portfolio if it is loaded with pictures that take a long time to download.

CHAPTER 2

Discovering Job Vacancies

There are several ways to find out about job vacancies. Some take a bit of work; others are a matter of "luck." In this chapter, we cover some of the ways you can improve your "luck" when scouting out job openings.

Right up front we'll tell you that you shouldn't limit your job search to only one or two sources. In this chapter we talk about ten ways to find teaching vacancies, five of which are accessible over the Internet:

- University career placement centers
- Job fairs
- Local and national newspaper advertisements
- School surveys
- Networking
- School district Web sites
- State department of education Web sites
- Your state's NEA affiliate's Web site
- Listservs
- General job-listing Web sites

The following sections discuss each of these sources of job-opening leads in detail.

University Career Placement Centers

If your college or university has a placement center, you should contact the staff as soon as possible. Placement services vary greatly from one school to another. Some colleges offer no placement services, others provide limited services, and some have well-staffed offices with surprisingly complete services. So consider yourself lucky if yours is the full-service type.

Historically, college placement offices have given special consideration to those in the teaching profession. Whereas these offices might maintain first-year placement files for graduates in most disciplines, many placement offices maintain placement files for teachers during their entire careers.

Of the teacher candidates in our survey, 50 percent said they had used the services of their university career placement centers.

If your college does not offer the services you need, check with other colleges. Some offer free services to part-time students, whereas others charge a reasonable fee. So it might be worth it, if it's practical to you, to sign up for a few classes at a university that does offer career services. This latter option becomes a consideration once you've decided where you want to teach. If you're looking for a position outside your immediate area, a college in that location might have job listings that aren't available through your own university.

A comprehensive placement program will offer several services, including the ones detailed in the following sections.

Offering Workshops and Counseling

Placement offices schedule workshops and offer counseling on various subjects:

- How to initiate your placement file
- Job-application procedures
- Ethics of the job search
- Interview techniques

These workshops usually are held in conjunction with your student-teaching program. Representatives from the placement office will coordinate these activities with classroom professors during your final year at the college.

Establishing Your Placement File

The placement office provides forms and procedures for establishing your placement file (also known as your professional file), which they then make available to potential employers at your request. You'll also need to provide letters of reference from professionals who observed you during your student-teaching phase, including your master teacher, college supervisor, school principal, and peers at the school where you taught. It's a good idea to ask for recommendations from people outside education as well, including former employers who can attest to your work ethic, dedication, and character. You should also ask for letters from people who are familiar with any youth-oriented volunteer service you have performed.

After you've landed a teaching position and have been teaching for a while, it's up to you to maintain your placement file. Keep the information current, including letters of reference from administrators and others at your school or district. In fact, ask for letters of reference every time you change positions, particularly from one school to another, or when your immediate supervisor is leaving his or her position for some reason. If you don't ask for these letters at the time, it might be difficult to get them later.

The important thing to remember is that future employers will want to know who you are and what you've done *lately*, not what you did ten years ago. A good rule of thumb is this: Unless a letter of reference can tell about something you've done that has "significantly altered the course of humankind," let it pass into your inactive file after several years, and replace it with a current letter.

Maintaining a Job-Related Reference Library

Placement-office libraries may contain information on schools throughout the world, including addresses, officials to contact, hiring procedures, and salary information. Particularly helpful are state school directories for the entire United States and some of the larger individual school districts. All of these directories contain valuable information for job seekers.

Maintaining Lists of Current Educational Job Vacancies

New job openings are usually posted on the placement office's bulletin board or added to a large three-ring binder. Some placement centers also send a weekly or monthly job listing to your home if you are willing to pay a subscription fee. Listings are generally for the immediate area around the college or university, but often you will see expanded lists of openings throughout the state, the country, and the world.

Tip: Many college placement offices maintain their own Web sites, where teaching vacancies are posted as soon as they pop up. These Web sites also offer helpful advice regarding the preparation of your resume and cover letter and important do's and don'ts of the interview process. If you're lucky, your placement office may also offer links to monsterTRAK.com and the OCC (Online Career Center). monsterTRAK.com is a great online listing of teaching vacancies that are posted daily with college career centers. OCC is another online service available to universities and colleges that offers extensive free nationwide job listings. You can search the list by geographic area or by using keywords.

Hosting Recruitment Interviews

Placement offices notify candidates of interview schedules for recruitment teams from visiting school districts, who might visit college campuses to recruit teachers. The frequency and number of these visits is determined by the job market and funding. If jobs are plentiful and teachers are scarce (as they were when this book was printed), expect to see more on-campus recruiting. If school districts have adequate funding, they expand their labor pool by searching college campuses for the best possible talent. Conversely, if teachers are in great supply or the districts are short on funds, don't expect to see many recruiters on campus.

Sending Your Placement File to Appropriate School Districts

Most college placement offices will send your placement file to school districts, but you need to familiarize yourself with your college's procedures. Some want the teacher candidate to initiate the request, whereas others want the request to come from school-district personnel. Some colleges offer this service at no cost, whereas others charge a fee.

Job Fairs

When it comes to job fairs, it appears that the exception *is* the rule. Formats and sponsors vary greatly; however, these fairs have a single purpose: to get job seekers together with prospective employers.

The most frequent sponsors of educational job fairs are the following:

> In our survey, 37 percent of the teacher candidates said they attended job fairs in their pursuit of teaching positions.

- **Large school districts:** Far and away the biggest sponsors of job fairs are the larger school districts. For a variety of reasons, larger districts are constantly in search of new teachers, and educational job fairs are one of the many ways they recruit these teachers.

- **County offices of education:** Another frequent sponsor of educational job fairs are county offices of education. One of the primary functions of these offices is to provide services and expertise to smaller schools within their counties, and job fairs provide a simple way to introduce teachers to these schools.

- **College placement centers:** Many college placement offices organize their own job fairs, at which several schools, districts, and county offices of education are represented.

- **Individual schools:** You occasionally find individual schools that set up booths at general job fairs. A general job fair includes a variety of corporate and government employers who are searching for employees with many different majors and degrees.

> "We hire about 50 percent of our teachers from job fairs and through university placement offices. The rest are hired through referrals from other teachers and administrators, unsolicited resumes, and from our substitute-teacher pool."
> —Bilingual resource specialist and member of the interview committee for a large urban school district in California

The format for educational job fairs varies. A teaching candidate might find school representatives actively screening files and conducting interviews for vacancies—and even hiring on the spot. More commonly, however, the representatives collect files and conduct informal interviews, with the goal of placing candidates in a hiring pool for consideration at a later date. Each school's or district's representative conducts a "show and tell" promotion, encouraging candidates to consider employment with that school or district.

Although educational job fairs can occur any time during the year, the vast majority take place between January and July. Watch for announcements of these fairs in your local newspaper and on your college placement office's bulletin board. You can also call various county offices of education or specific school districts and ask whether they have fairs scheduled.

We encourage you to participate in at least one large educational job fair in your area. This is a valuable way to sell yourself to prospective employers and learn more about the available opportunities.

Whenever you attend a job fair, be sure to bring along extra copies of your resume, your college placement file, evidence of teaching certificates, your demonstration video, your portfolio, and a list of questions to ask each representative.

Your personal appearance is important, so dress the same way you would for a formal, scheduled interview. After each job fair, send thank-you notes to the representatives of any schools or districts where you plan to formally pursue employment.

Local and National Newspaper Advertisements

Keep an eye on newspaper ads. You'll be surprised how many up-to-date job vacancies are listed regularly, not only in your local paper, but nationally. What many teacher candidates don't realize is that many national newspapers advertise teaching positions all over the country and overseas. For example, the *New York Times* is a great source of possibilities.

Most newspaper job ads for teaching vacancies include codes that indicate certain characteristics about the job vacancy:

- **Cert:** A teaching certificate is required.
- **Dual cert:** Two types of certification are required.
- **EOE:** Equal Opportunity Employer (the district does not discriminate, in accordance with federal and state mandates).
- **FTE:** The position is some type of full-time employment, although not necessarily a full-time position. You need to inquire how many hours per day are required.
- **LR:** This indicates a leave replacement, which is a temporary position until the teacher taking leave returns.
- **PT:** This indicates a part-time position.
- **PDS:** This position is a substitute who will be paid by the day.
- **PS:** This position is a substitute who will serve as a permanent substitute, which means that he or she will probably be paid a lower salary than a regularly employed certificated teacher.
- **PB:** This is a probationary position that might eventually become tenured after the term of probation has been successfully served.

After you've located a few job vacancies that sound interesting, go to the Web sites of the school districts advertising the positions. There you'll find more detailed information about the position and the district itself. If a certain position is open at only a specific school within the district, click the link on the district's Web site that tells you all about that school.

If you're still interested in the job, go to the Web site for your state board of education, and access the link called "School Report Cards." With only a couple of clicks, you'll be able to read the school "report card" for the specific school where the position exists. Isn't the Internet a marvelous tool? As the Russian comedian Yakov Smirnoff would say, "What a country!"

School Surveys

School surveys are a smart way to discover job vacancies before they're advertised and to shop yourself around. They also help you discover which schools are a fit for you—which ones dovetail with your mission statement. You conduct these surveys in person, as cold calls. You simply drop by the offices of any schools or districts that interest you, whether or not they have any current vacancies.

 Note: School survey calls should be made *in person,* not over the phone.

Although only 13 percent of the teacher candidates we talked with conducted school surveys, we think they are *a must.* Here's why: Although almost all teaching vacancies must, by law, be advertised, you're at a great advantage if you know about them ahead of time. There are other ways to find them, of course—through networking (which we'll talk about later in this chapter) or by being in the right place at the right time. But one excellent way to hear of vacancies before they're advertised is to conduct your own school surveys. The following sections show you how to go about it.

"A wise man will make more opportunities than he finds."
—Francis Bacon

Make a List of the Schools and Districts That Interest You

By this time you probably have some idea of the schools at which you might like to teach. Maybe you heard about them from your professors, friends, or relatives, or maybe you really liked the school where you did your student teaching. One consideration is how far the school is from your home. Only you know how far you are willing to drive to work each day, or if you're willing to move to another city.

Be sure to consider *all* the schools in your area. There might be schools you are unfamiliar with, or private or religious schools you might consider. Or you might hear of a school through your network. The important thing is not to limit yourself to schools with "friendly faces"—people you already know or have met. Most of your contacts will be cold calls, and *that's okay!* By leaving your comfort zone and reaching beyond the friendly faces, you'll uncover openings your competitors haven't heard about.

Rank Your List

After you've made your list of possible target schools, organize it by placing your first choices at the top. To help prioritize your list, you can use *school report cards.* This sheet of information tells about the school's mission statement, philosophy, ethnic profile, test scores, attendance records, expenditures per student, class sizes, facilities, services offered, teacher-evaluation policies, discipline policies, textbooks and instructional materials used, and salaries. Not all schools offer report cards to the public, but many states require that schools make these reports available. If you can get your hands on one of these report cards for each school you plan to visit, you'll have a world of information at your fingertips that will help you prioritize your visits as well as give you valuable information that will come in handy in interviews.

We have included a sample school report card from a high school in Arizona (see figure 2.1).

Ironwood High School

ARIZONA SCHOOL REPORT CARD 2003-04

6051 W. Sweetwater, Glendale, AZ 85304
Peoria Unified School District

Arizona's report cards have been revised to include requirements in the federal No Child Left Behind Act, such as Adequate Yearly Progress and the disaggregation of student level data into required subgroups.

AZ LEARNS[1]

High School Achievement Profile *

Performing*

* The profiles are Excelling, Highly Performing, Performing or Underperforming.

No Child Left Behind

Adequate Yearly Progress***

Met

School Improvement Status***

N/A

*** For additional information, please refer to the AYP page in this report card.

School Overview

Principal/Administrator :	Mr. Mark Matheson
Schedule :	7:00 AM to 3:30 PM
Grades :	9-12
2003 Enrollment :	2171
Web Address :	www.peoriaud.k12.az.us
Phone Number :	(623) 486-6400
Fax Number :	(623) 486-6424
E-mail :	mmathesonpeoriaud.k12.az.us

Mission

Provide outstanding programs and opportunities for all students to be responsible citizens and lifelong learners in a changing world. Ironwood High School exists for the benefit of each student regardless of his/her capacity for learning.

School / Academic Goals

- Ironwood students will apply higher-level thinking skills to a variety of relevant situations.

- Ironwood students will demonstrate improvement in reading comprehension and vocabulary, oral presentations and written expression.

Instructional Programs

- Honors Classes
- International Baccalaureate
- On-site Special Education
- Advanced Placement

Enrollment

October 1, 2002 School Year Student Enrollment :	2104
Accepting New Students in 2003-04 Under Open Enrollment Law[2] :	No
Number of Students Attending Under Open Enrollment in 2002-03 :	175

Calendar Information

Number of Instruction Days :	178
Average Daily Instruction Time :	6 hours 30 minutes
First Day of School :	8/11/2003
Last Day of School :	5/20/2004

Visit http://www.ade.az.gov/azlearns/ for more information on the performance of your school.

Financial information will be posted on the web in early 2004 after schools have completed year-end reports.

ARIZONA
DEPARTMENT OF
EDUCATION

Figure 2.1: A sample school report card.

(continued)

(continued)

Ironwood High School

School Site Council

Council Composition	Council Duties
1 School Administrator(s)	• Parent/Educator Relations
1 Non-certified Employee(s)	• Community Communication
2 Teacher(s)	• Voter Information
6 Parent(s)	• School Safety
2 Community Member(s)	
2 Student(s)	

Staffing Information for School Year 2003-04

Position	Number	Position	Number
Administrator	4.00	Teacher	111.00
Other Professional Staff	.00	Teacher Aide	7.00

Educational Attainment by Years of Teaching Experience for School Year 2003-04

Experience	Bachelor's	Master's	Doctorate	Other
3 or fewer years	30	5	0	0
4 to 6 years	13	10	10	0
7 to 9 years	11	0	1	0
10 or more years	26	23	1	0

Shared Responsibilities

School

Provide all students with the best learning environment and the best opportunities to learn. In addition to providing safe, attractive school campuses, each school invites and maintains high parent involvement.

Parents

Parents have the responsibility to act in partnership with the school and work cooperatively with staff members to educate their children. This includes supporting student attendance, modeling positive attitudes toward learning and fostering respect.

Resources Available at School Site

Special Facilities

• Media Production Studio   • PASS Lab

Extracurricular Activities

• National Honor Society   • Distinguished Scholar Program

• Performing Arts Programs   • Variety of Service Clubs

Social Services

• Counseling Services   • Crisis Intervention

• Job Placement Services   • Adult Education

Transportation Policy

Transportation is provided for all eligible students who reside beyond two miles of Ironwood High School. Additionally, transportation services are provided for eligible special education students to Ironwood High School.

Ironwood High School

Indicators of Success Based on Historical Data from 2002-03

School Achievements/Accomplishments 2002-03

- All teachers document instruction in higher-level thinking skills during annual formal evaluations. Approximately 50 AP, Honors and AIM classes average 24 students per class. Scholar athlete teams; Golden Bell Award for Distinguished Scholar Program.

- Course assessments include writing across the curriculum. Students earn multiple scholarships and are accepted to prestigious universities. Flinn Scholar; Voice of Democracy; Aeirie Writing Magazine; District Poetry Winners; Journalism Awards.

School Honors

Awards or Special Recognition Received By the School, Staff or Students

Award/Honor	Year
• National Hispanic Scholars	2002
• America's Best High Schools	1996
• Flinn Scholar	2000
• National Merit Scholars - Semi-finalist	2003

Student Activity Rates for School Year 2002-03

	% School	% K-6	Arizona % 7-8	% 9-12
Attendance Rate [2]	98	95	94	96
Transfers Out [3]	14	20	20	20
Transfers In[4] (Within District)	0	2	2	2
Transfers In[5] (Out of District)	5	10	10	9
Promotion Rate [6]	99	99	98	95
Retention Rate [7]	1	1	2	5
Dropout Rate [8]	1			8
Status Unknown [9]	1			6
Graduation Rate[10]	95			76

Measure of Academic Progress

No MAP data found for this school.

The MAP is an elementary school (Grades 2-8) indicator only.

Arizona's Measure of Academic Progress (MAP) is an indicator of student academic growth from one year to the next. The results are based on the Stanford Achievement Test, Ninth Edition (Stanford 9), given in 2002-03. MAP includes only those students who were tested both years in consecutive grade levels at the same school or who started the school year in the same school in which they were tested in 2003. A student achieves One Year's Growth (OYG) if he or she remains in the same Stanine or advances a Stanine from one year to the next. The percentage of students achieving OYG at the school is reported above.

NC = Not Calculated (less than 10 matches)   Dashes (--) = No Data Available

Stanines are normalized standard scores that range from a low of 1 to a high of 9, with 5 designating average performance. National Stanines, like National Percentile Ranks, indicate a student's relative standing in the national norm group (Source: Harcourt Educational Measurement).

(continued)

(continued)

Ironwood High School

Arizona's Instrument to Measure Standards (AIMS) Results 2002-03 [11]
10th Grade

Mathematics	# Tested			% Tested			MSS			% FFB			% A			% Met			% Exceeded		
	S	D	AZ	S	D	AZ	S	D	AZ	S	D	AZ	S	D	AZ	S	D	AZ	S	D	AZ
All Students	485	2474	57534	91	92	91	500	500	491	32	32	46	22	21	16	29	30	23	17	16	15
All Students (Prior Year)	479	2262	51010	NA	NA	NA	491	492	483	33	31	45	29	32	20	28	28	23	10	9	11
Female	243	1236	28155	92	93	90	501	501	491	28	30	47	22	23	16	33	31	24	17	16	14
Male	239	1230	28932	89	91	89	499	500	491	36	34	46	21	19	15	26	30	23	16	17	16
African American	16	123	2558	84	92	86	491	490	475	47	47	64	13	18	15	33	28	16	7	8	6
Hispanic	76	447	17547	84	91	86	488	491	475	43	43	64	25	22	15	28	27	15	4	9	6
Asian/Pacific Islander	21	83	1395	88	93	96	527	513	519	6	18	22	17	22	16	28	26	28	50	33	35
American Indian/Alaskan Native	NC	20	3794	NC	111	91	NC	495	468	NC	38	72	NC	8	13	NC	38	12	NC	15	3
White	369	1791	29790	93	92	86	501	503	501	31	29	34	22	22	17	30	31	29	18	18	20
Students with Disabilities	32	177	5562	82	83	93	NA	468	461	NA	33	79	NA	67	10	NA	0	8	NA	0	3
Students without Disabilities	453	2297	51972	92	93	90	500	500	492	32	32	45	22	21	16	29	30	24	17	16	15
Limited English Proficient Students	13	65	5467	650	271	111	NA	501	458	NA	0	87	NA	50	7	NA	50	1	NA	0	1
Migrant Students	--	NC	702				--	NC	471	--	NC	74	--	NC	9	--	NC	14	--	NC	3
Economically Disadvantaged	--	NC	10446				--	NC	472	--	NC	70	--	NC	13	--	NC	13	--	NC	4
Non-Economically Disadvantaged	485	2471	47088				500	500	495	32	32	42	22	21	16	29	30	26	17	16	15

Reading	# Tested			% Tested			MSS			% FFB			% A			% Met			% Exceeded		
	S	D	AZ	S	D	AZ	S	D	AZ	S	D	AZ	S	D	AZ	S	D	AZ	S	D	AZ
All Students	477	2399	56700	90	89	89	522	519	512	7	9	15	20	21	23	61	60	52	13	11	10
All Students (Prior Year)	495	2308	50525	NA	NA	NA	526	526	517	6	5	12	16	18	22	63	60	51	15	17	15
Female	242	1208	27862	91	91	89	527	524	517	4	6	12	19	18	22	63	64	54	14	12	12
Male	233	1184	28398	87	87	88	517	513	507	10	12	19	21	23	24	57	56	49	12	9	9
African American	17	117	2529	85	87	85	505	508	495	19	11	24	25	26	31	50	57	41	6	5	4
Hispanic	80	438	17305	90	89	85	504	506	494	15	13	24	27	28	31	56	55	44	1	4	4
Asian/Pacific Islander	20	80	1382	83	90	95	546	531	530	0	6	6	6	14	17	76	65	59	18	14	17
American Indian/Alaskan Native	NC	19	3815	NC	106	91	NC	517	489	NC	15	29	NC	23	35	NC	46	35	NC	15	2
White	358	1725	29209	90	88	84	525	522	525	5	7	9	19	19	17	61	61	59	15	12	15
Students with Disabilities	24	151	5215	62	71	87	NA	489	478	NA	25	43	NA	50	29	NA	25	25	NA	0	2
Students without Disabilities	453	2248	51485	92	91	89	522	519	513	7	9	15	20	21	23	61	60	52	13	11	11
Limited English Proficient Students	13	60	5378	650	250	109	NA	531	471	NA	0	48	NA	0	36	NA	100	15	NA	0	0
Migrant Students	--	NC	689				--	NC	486	--	NC	36	--	NC	36	--	NC	30	--	NC	2
Economically Disadvantaged	--	NC	10358				--	NC	492	--	NC	26	--	NC	33	--	NC	37	--	NC	4
Non-Economically Disadvantaged	477	2396	46342				522	519	516	7	9	14	20	21	21	61	60	54	13	11	12

Writing	# Tested			% Tested			MSS			% FFB			% A			% Met			% Exceeded		
	S	D	AZ	S	D	AZ	S	D	AZ	S	D	AZ	S	D	AZ	S	D	AZ	S	D	AZ
All Students	494	2499	55090	93	93	87	498	490	479	6	8	16	9	12	13	85	81	70	0	0	0
All Students (Prior Year)	460	2257	50572	NA	NA	NA	498	492	481	4	6	14	25	21	23	71	73	63	0	0	1
Female	248	1275	27752	94	96	89	504	496	483	5	6	13	7	7	9	87	85	75	0	0	0
Male	243	1216	26842	91	90	83	493	484	474	7	10	20	10	14	15	83	76	65	0	0	0
African American	15	122	2336	75	91	78	485	474	464	14	16	25	7	12	14	79	72	62	0	0	0
Hispanic	80	432	16391	90	88	81	481	477	458	13	14	28	8	11	16	79	75	56	0	0	0
Asian/Pacific Islander	22	87	1356	92	98	93	525	499	499	0	3	7	0	8	9	100	89	83	0	0	2
American Indian/Alaskan Native	NC	20	3731	NC	111	89	NC	455	446	NC	38	37	NC	6	16	NC	56	47	NC	0	0
White	372	1815	29053	93	93	84	501	494	492	4	6	10	10	12	12	86	82	79	0	0	0
Students with Disabilities	30	144	4141	77	68	69	400	427	436	100	62	47	0	8	18	0	31	35	0	0	0
Students without Disabilities	464	2355	50949	94	95	89	499	491	479	6	7	16	9	12	13	85	81	71	0	0	0
Limited English Proficient Students	13	58	4711	650	242	96	NA	496	422	NA	0	61	NA	0	13	NA	100	26	NA	0	0
Migrant Students	--	NC	666				--	NC	444	--	NC	39	--	NC	11	--	NC	50	--	NC	0
Economically Disadvantaged	--	NC	10168				--	NC	453	--	NC	32	--	NC	14	--	NC	54	--	NC	0
Non-Economically Disadvantaged	494	2498	44922				498	490	484	6	8	13	9	12	13	85	81	73	0	0	0

NC = Not Calculated (less than 10 students) Dashes (--) = No Data Available NA = Not Applicable S = School D = District

District brochures can be very revealing as well. You can pick up a district's brochure by calling or visiting its personnel office. Figure 2.2 is a sample brochure from the Mt. Diablo Unified School District in California.

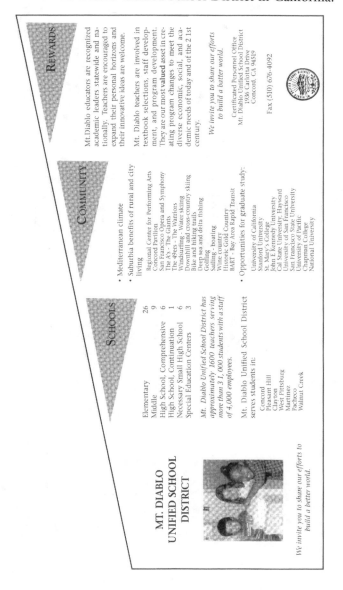

(continued)

Figure 2.2: A sample school district brochure.

(continued)

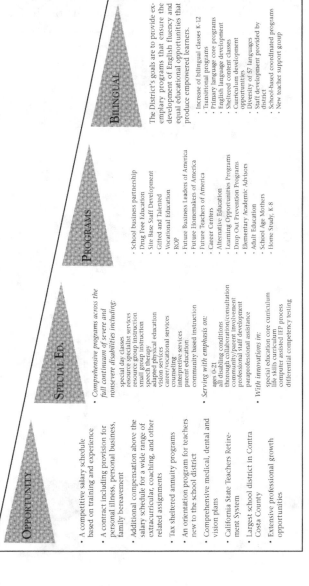

OPPORTUNITY

- A competitive salary schedule based on training and experience
- A contract including provision for personal illness, personal business, family bereavement
- Additional compensation above the salary schedule for a wide range of extracurricular, coaching, and other related assignments
- Tax sheltered annuity programs
- An orientation program for teachers new to the school district
- Comprehensive medical, dental and vision plans
- California State Teachers Retirement System
- Largest school district in Contra Costa County
- Extensive professional growth opportunities

SPECIAL ED.

- *Comprehensive programs across the full continuum of severe and nonsevere disabilities including:*
  - special day classes
  - resource specialist services
  - resource group instruction
  - small group instruction
  - speech therapy
  - adapted physical education
  - vision services
  - career/vocational services
  - counseling
  - interpretive services
  - parent education
  - community based instruction
- *Serving with emphasis on:*
  - ages 0-21
  - all disabling conditions
  - thorough collaboration/consultation
  - community/parent involvement
  - professional staff development
  - paraprofessional assistance
- *With innovations in:*
  - special education core curriculum
  - life skills curriculum
  - computer assisted IEP process
  - differential competency testing

PROGRAMS

- School business partnership
- Drug Free Education
- Site Base Staff Development
- Gifted and Talented
- Vocational Education
- ROP
- Future Business Leaders of America
- Future Homemakers of America
- Future Teachers of America
- Career Centers
- Alternative Education
- Learning Opportunities Programs
- Drop Out Prevention Programs
- Elementary Academic Advisors
- Adult Education
- School Age Mothers
- Home Study, K-8

BILINGUAL

The District's goals are to provide exemplary programs that ensure the development of English fluency and equal educational opportunities that produce empowered learners.

- Increase of bilingual classes K-12
- Transitional programs
- Primary language core programs
- English language development
- Sheltered content classes
- Curriculum development opportunities
- Diversity of 57 languages
- Staff development provided by district
- School-based coordinated programs
- New teacher support group

Set Up a Cold-Calling Schedule

If you're like most people, you procrastinate. Even if you agree that it's
smart to conduct school surveys as
part of your job search, it takes discipline to get yourself out there and
pound the pavement—especially
because it means getting dressed
and groomed for a possible interview. So we suggest that you set
up a calling schedule of a certain
number of cold calls per week. If
you hope to start teaching in the

> "Starting in March or April, a candidate should make contact with every district he or she can conceive of working at. This process of cold calling, sending resumes, and follow-ing up continues through the end of September… openings pop up constantly. The individual who sends the fax first, after finding out about a position before it has been advertised, wins points for eagerness."
>
> —High school music teacher in New Jersey

fall, for example, you should begin your schedule in early spring,
methodically calling on schools or district offices.

Don't give up if your first call doesn't produce a job lead; keep going back until
your face is engraved in the minds of your contacts at each school. You never
know. A position might become vacant at the last minute, even after the school
year has started, so never give up.

Begin Making Your Calls

Although cold calling might seem intimidating, you should realize that most
people are *happy* to talk to you and brag about their school or district.
Everyone—including the school secretary, the custodian, teachers' aides, bus
drivers, teachers, administrators, and those who work in the personnel office—
will be impressed with your eagerness to become known and to find out more
about them. You'll find that the more cold calls you make, the easier they
become, and the more encouraged you'll be.

Some of your calls may result in an informal visit with the principal or personnel director. Or you might be given the name of someone else to contact, perhaps at the district office. In any case, keep in mind that your ultimate goal is to
make personal contact with someone who has *hiring power*. Although your first
contact will usually be with a school secretary or someone who works at the
district personnel office, ask to speak with the principal, personnel director, or
anyone who sits on the hiring panel.

Make your calls with the expectation of talking to one of these key people that
day. This means you should treat the process in much the same way you would
treat a scheduled interview. That is, be prepared to make a good impression
when it comes to your dress, grooming, body language, eye contact, handshake,

and attitude (we'll talk more about this in chapter 7). This isn't a formal interview, however, and you should be prepared to explain the purpose of your visit. Here's an example of what you might say:

"My name is _____, and I'm looking for a position as a classroom teacher. I'm interested in your school district because of its excellent reputation. I plan to apply for any positions that become available, but today I was just hoping to meet you and learn more about your school district."

By cold calling in advance of job announcements and meeting the principal (or anyone else who sits on the hiring panel), you're guaranteed to impress. Many of the administrators we interviewed said that when it came time to schedule interviews, they remembered which candidates had made the early calls, and they could match faces with the names on those applications.

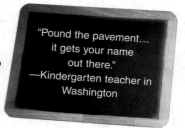

"Pound the pavement… it gets your name out there."
—Kindergarten teacher in Washington

By the way, it's a good idea to bring your portfolio along on these calls, just in case you're given a chance to "show and tell." Also have one of your demo videos handy, and offer to leave it with anyone who will agree to take it.

Remember, the purpose of a school survey is twofold: Not only are you looking for a school that's a perfect fit for you, but, equally important, you're trying to become *known.* You've probably heard that it's who you know that counts. Every contact you make through cold calling enlists another important person who now *knows* you.

It keeps coming back to the Madison Avenue idea of marketing and selling your product—*you!*

Keep Track of Your Contacts

You need to keep a record of your contacts. Use the following form as a guide; you'll need one sheet per school or district.

School Survey

Name of school or district:_____

Address:_____

Phone number: _____

Web site: _____

Date of first contact: _____

Name and title of person contacted: _____

Upcoming vacancies (if any): _____

_____

Materials received from the school or district: _____

_____

School report card? _____

District brochure? _____

Notices of current vacancies? _____

Application? _____

Other:_____

Material given to the school or district: _____

Resume? _____

Letters of reference? _____

Demo video? _____

Other:_____

Follow-up

Second visit? _____

_____

_____

Date: _____

Name and title of person contacted: _____

Returned application? _____

Date: _____

Had college placement file sent: _____

Date: _____

Other follow-up contacts: _____

_____

Comments and impressions of the school district: _____

_____

_____

_____

Network, Network, Network!

Networking has become more than a buzzword in today's corporate job market; it's now essential for job applicants in all professions, including teaching, to get their "net" working in every way possible. To do this, you should talk to anyone and everyone, anytime and anywhere, in the hope of discovering a job vacancy or making contact with someone who has hiring authority.

This concept has been adopted in the field of education over the past decade or so, along with other job search strategies borrowed from the corporate world (such as the use of a portfolio and demo video). When it comes to networking, however, teachers have an advantage over people in many other professions because of the built-in network that exists in the educational community.

For example, by the time you've completed your student teaching, you'll already have a net full of influential contacts: professors, school principals, mentor teachers, master teachers, and other teachers with whom you have worked. Don't forget friends and relatives. Remind them to keep an eye out for openings in their communities. And if you've been working on your school surveys, you have an excellent network of contacts there as well.

> In our survey, 51 percent of the teacher candidates networked throughout their communities in their search for job leads and contacts.

Many teacher candidates have done some substitute teaching, resulting in even more contacts. If you distinguish yourself during your substitute or student-teaching experiences, many of your contacts will be happy to recommend you to a "hire" authority or will apprise you of upcoming openings.

If you're introduced to an administrator or personnel director, treat the meeting as you would a school survey. You might not be involved in an official interview at this meeting, but your purpose is to let this person know who you are and that you are interested in any future openings. Even if nothing is available at the moment, you never know when a position will open up in the future. At that time, you might be invited for a formal interview. At the very least, you can say that someone with the authority and power to hire you now knows who you are. The networking contacts you establish within the educational community are invaluable—treasure them!

> "Talk to everyone you know or meet who is in the field of education about your job search."
> —High school English teacher in Texas

You should network outside the educational community as well, through face-to-face contacts and the liberal use of the phone, voice mail, e-mail, and fax machines. Ask everyone you come into contact with if they know someone with hiring power in the local schools, or if they know of an upcoming teaching vacancy. If you make it a point to network with people every day, you'll be surprised at the leads you'll turn up. For example, you might be paired at the golf course with a member of the school board, or your teller at the bank might know of an opening at her daughter's school.

> The more people you meet and talk to about teaching vacancies, the more chances you have of landing a job.

Talk to everyone: members of your church, your dentist, your fellow health nuts at the fitness club. Although we don't recommend it, we know one teacher who even customized the message on her answering machine:

> _"This is Cindy, the desperate, out-of-work teacher. Leave all your job leads at the beep."_

It might have been better to say this instead:

> _"This is Cindy, the skilled and experienced educator. I am currently available for a new teaching position. Leave all your job leads at the beep."_

It's a fact that many more people find jobs through networking than they do through conventional job search methods.

Tip: You can network within the school where you are working as a student teacher, substitute teacher, temporary teacher, or volunteer. This type of networking is such an important way to find a plum teaching position that we've devoted an entire chapter to the subject. See chapter 4 for effective ways to network within the school itself.

Use the Internet

The Internet is an exciting, innovative, and effective way to find and apply for job vacancies. Not only does the Internet offer hundreds of places to search for available teaching positions, but it also provides an electronic avenue for filling out applications, sending your resume, and conducting interviews by e-mail.

An overwhelming percentage of American college students have free access to the Internet, and a high percentage of them plan to take advantage of this access to conduct an electronic job search.

Obviously, as more people sign onto the Net every day, the percentages will grow. If you don't have the luxury of free Internet access, you can sign on through one of the commercial providers (such as Prodigy or America Online) or through any other provider that offers unlimited direct access for a flat monthly rate.

If you've spent any time surfing the Net, you know that whatever you're searching for is never all together in one place. If you're looking for teaching vacancies, you'll find them scattered all over cyberspace. The following sections describe some of the best places to begin your search.

School District Web Sites

This is the easiest way to stay abreast of job vacancies in your favorite districts. If you don't know a certain district's Web address, you can find it on one of the search engines, such as www.google.com, by searching for the name of the district in quotation marks. Usually, the district's site will appear at the top of the list of "finds." Click the link to access its home page with information galore. For example, the home page for the Tucson (Arizona) Unified School District (www.tusd.k12.az.us) includes links to more information, such as the following:

- Job openings
- District information
- School information
- School newsletters
- Curricula
- Professional development
- Calendar
- Departments
- News and events
- Student guidelines
- TUSD statistics
- School boundary maps
- Board agenda

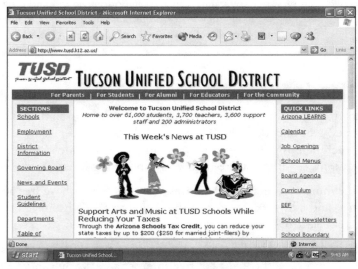

Figure 2.3: The Tucson Unified School District's home page.

The TUSD's Web site is a wonderful example of a professionally maintained site with up-to-date links. For example, when we clicked the Job Openings link, we found detailed job descriptions for counselors, special education teachers, general elementary teachers, resource teacher, librarian, and many others.

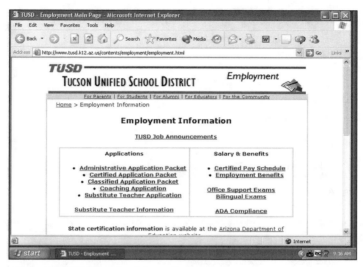

Figure 2.4: TUSD's online job-posting page.

When we clicked the link to District Information, we found nearly 40 more links, one per subject, such as Parents' FAQ, Afterschool Programs, School Boundary Maps, Progress Report, Budget, CORE Curriculum, Graduation Requirements, TUSD Creed, District Priorities, and TUSD Timeline.

When we clicked the Schools link, we chose a specific elementary school whose link gave us all the specifics about the school, including the number of students, the year the school opened, the grades served, the school's hours, special achieve-ments, special programs, and the name of the principal.

If you discover a teaching vacancy at a specific school, and the district Web site does not include the school's report card, you can find it by accessing the Web site for your state department of education (see the appendix).

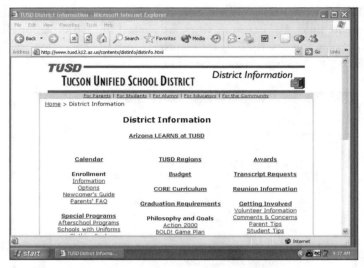

Figure 2.5: Online information about the school district.

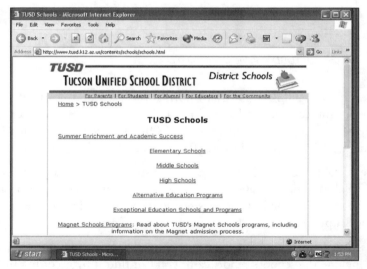

Figure 2.6: Information about a specific school in the district.

State Department of Education Web Sites

Most state department of education Web sites now include a jobs link that lists all the teaching positions available in the state. The appendix includes detailed contact information for every state department of education in the United States, including their Web site addresses. Keep an eye on your state's site for job vacancies as they become available.

NEA State Affiliate Web Sites

The National Education Association (NEA) is the leading organization in the United States for the advancement of public education. Each state has an NEA affiliate that offers valuable information. You can learn about news in education or employment opportunities in each state through its NEA affiliate. See the appendix for each state affiliate's Web site address.

Listservs

Listservs are discussion groups geared toward very specific types of people. Dozens of listservs target educators. These listservs provide a kind of support group for teachers and administrators. Members of these groups send e-mails that are posted so that everyone can read them, reply to them, or print them for their files. These listservs often include job vacancies listed by school districts. They also give you an opportunity to post your resume, with the hope that it will be read by someone on a hiring panel who will request further information.

To locate a teacher-related listserv, go to your favorite search engine and enter "listserv directories," which will bring up several sites that offer listserv directories. Or go to http://tile.net/search.php and enter "teacher" in the Search box at the bottom left of the page.

Job Web Sites

Many free and fee-based job Web sites exist. Here are a few of the most popular job Web sites that list teaching vacancies:

http://jobs.teachers.net/data/
    jobcenter/
www.careerbuilder.com
    (lists national newspaper
    want ads)
www.K12jobs.com

www.recruitingteachers.org
www.teachers-teachers.com
www.usteach.com
www.wanttoteach.com

A Few Words of Advice About Job Searching Over the Internet

Here are some tips that will help you get the most out of your online job search:

- **Follow directions to the letter,** whether you're applying online to a school district directly, posting your resume on a listserv, or applying through an online job site. Don't "wing it"—they're watching to see whether you can follow instructions!

- **Watch your grammar and spelling.** It's so easy to get a little sloppy when filling out applications online, sending e-mail messages, or posting resumes and cover letters. E-mail gets you used to writing casual, informal messages in which anything goes—misspelled words, poor grammar, and so on. So, be extra careful as you apply online. In fact, have someone proofread your work for spelling or grammar problems.

- **Be aware of attachment issues.** When attaching any document, such as a cover letter or your resume, to an e-mail or an online application, always specify in the body of the e-mail or application what type of word-processing system was used to create your attachments. And if the job posting specifies "no attachments," you must paste your resume into the body of the e-mail as plain text and proof it for the formatting problems that might result. (For example, boldfacing and bullets will disappear, and long lines of text will break in funny places.)

- **Be careful when posting your resume.** Posting your resume on the Internet is a little different from sending a sheet of paper through the mail. An online resume is shown on a computer screen that has about 20 available lines, so it can be a smart idea to limit your resume to a single screen. Many experts are finding, however, that viewers don't seem to mind scrolling through a resume as long as it isn't too lengthy.

- **Be careful when filling out an application online.** If your job search generates interest from a school district, you might be able to fill out your application and send it by e-mail. Fill out the application according to the instructions, and then proofread it for any spelling or grammar errors. If your application makes a positive impression, you might receive a telephone call—or you might be interviewed by e-mail as well. The ultimate goal, of course, is to receive an invitation to interview in person. E-mail applications and interviews are more common when you are searching for a job in another state or overseas.

If you're a "newbie" to cyberspace, everything we've written here might just as well have been in a foreign language. You need to locate a good book on browsing the Internet and, more specifically, on searching for a job online. One of the best is *Best Career and Education Web Sites,* by Anne Wolfinger (JIST Publishing).

Tip: Once you've located one or more positions that interest you, don't dally about getting your letter and resume in the mail. If the position is listed as an immediate vacancy, make a couple of phone calls and, if possible, fax or e-mail your application, along with your resume and, possibly, your digital portfolio. By the way, whenever you fax your application, *always* follow up with a "snail mail" application as well (faxes have a way of getting lost!).

Whenever an unexpected vacancy pops up—due to a sudden illness or death of a teacher, for example—the school administrator needs to fill that position ASAP. So be the first candidate to apply, and rush to the interview, if one is offered.

CHAPTER 3

Making the Paper Cut: Resumes, Cover Letters, Applications, and Letters of Reference

You won't be hired without an interview, and you won't be interviewed unless you make the paper cut—a school district's initial screening process that determines whether you'll be asked to interview. Because it's so important for you to make this cut, it's crucial that you understand the concept.

To begin with, the "paper" we're referring to here includes all the pieces of paper you submit to a school district in your pursuit of a teaching position. Depending on the district's requirements, these may include a resume, letters of reference, an application, a cover letter, copies of your college transcripts, or information forwarded from your placement file.

Every school district has its own paper-screening philosophy. This chapter describes some of the most common. Then we show you how to put together an impressive resume and cover letter, how to fill out the schools' application forms, and how to get and present an excellent set of references.

Screening Procedures

Many larger school districts use a process whereby one elementary and one secondary principal are designated to screen applicants' papers at their respective grade levels. During this initial screening, the better papers are placed in an active file (or applicant pool) for a certain period of time, usually one school year. This applicant pool is used as a resource when a teaching vacancy occurs anywhere in the district or when there's a need to hire a long-term substitute.

The poorer papers are either discarded or placed in an inactive file, where they're seldom (or never) seen again. This inactive file is usually discarded at the end of each school year.

When a specific teaching vacancy occurs, it is advertised. Any applications or resumes received as a result are sent to the particular school's site administrator (usually the principal) for screening, along with the resumes in the district's active file. The site administrator then chooses the top five or ten applicants.

Depending on the school district's philosophy, these applications might be referred to an interview team for further screening before interviews are scheduled, or the site administrator might decide which of the candidates will be scheduled for interviews. Shared decision making is a popular philosophy these days, especially among the larger school districts, although some districts place great emphasis on giving the school's principal sole decision-making power.

An interview team, by the way, usually consists of the site administrator, teachers, parents, and school-board members or community residents. An interview might be conducted by an interview team (also known as an *interview committee* or a *hiring panel*) or solely by the site administrator.

Many large school districts have well-staffed personnel departments that do the initial screening of all applicants, whether they're applying for current or future vacancies. The personnel director and his or her staff make the first paper cut, placing the top applicants for each type of vacancy in active files that are delivered to the principals at schools where specific vacancies exist. The principals choose the top candidates from these prescreened files to be scheduled for interviews with a hiring panel or with the principal.

Smaller school districts often bypass these initial screenings and refer all applicants' files directly to the principal at the school where an opening exists. This administrator does all the work: screens the files, makes the paper cut, and schedules the top candidates for interviews.

Whatever the district's philosophy, however, you won't be scheduled for an interview unless your file makes it past the initial screening process. Our goal is to help you do just that.

Teacher-Specific Resumes

Many excellent books are available on resume writing. One in particular stands out: *Expert Resumes for Teachers and Educators,* Second Edition, by Wendy Enelow and Louise Kursmark (JIST Publishing, 2005). Several sample resumes from this book are included in this chapter to give you an idea of what an excellent teacher resume looks like. We'll also share our tips for writing an outstanding teacher resume that gets you past the initial screening and helps you get that all-important face-to-face interview with the hiring officials.

Writing an Outstanding Resume

You might never have needed a resume until now, and the very thought of writing one might seem overwhelming. Your fears are understandable, but we guarantee that you'll feel much better about the whole thing after you've read through this section. We've tried to simplify the process of resume writing by giving you some clear, concise direction in a question-and-answer format.

What Is a Resume?

A resume is a concise, easy-to-read history of your life that includes your job objective, educational background, employment history, community service, work skills, and accomplishments. A resume (along with the application and letters of reference) is the tool most district personnel use to screen teacher candidates before scheduling interviews.

Why Is a Resume Important?

A resume is one of the most important tools you'll use in your job search. It represents you and indicates who you are. An outstanding, flawless resume can eventually land you an interview; likewise, a poorly written, sloppy resume will kill your chances. An effective resume should include the information most likely to impress the particular school or district to which you are applying. If you impress the screeners with your resume, as well as with your application and letters of reference, they'll schedule you for an interview, and you'll have made the paper cut. Unless you survive this initial screening process, you'll never make it to the interview table.

How Long Should a Resume Be?

If you're a recent college graduate with limited work experience, a one-page resume is ideal. If you have extensive related work experience, however, a page and a half to two pages should be the limit. If your resume is longer than one page, you run the risk that only the first page will be read, especially if the personnel office is swamped with applicants.

What Are the Common Resume Formats, and What Is the Difference Between Them?

There are three basic resume formats: *chronological, functional,* and *combination.* Depending on your background and experience, one format might be better for presenting your qualifications than another:

- **Chronological resumes** list your employment experience in reverse-chronological order, starting with your most recent position and working backward in time.

Advantages: Easy to write, easy to read, and widely accepted by school-district personnel.

Disadvantages: Not a good choice if you have little or no work history, if you've been a job hopper or are changing careers, or if you have had long lapses between employment.

- **Functional resumes**, also known as *skills resumes,* emphasize your skills, strengths, and accomplishments.

    Advantages: A popular choice for recent college graduates and career switchers. Provides a practical format for selling yourself by accentuating your strengths and transferable skills.

    Disadvantages: Difficult to organize and read unless very well formatted. Many employers see the use of this format as a red flag that the candidate has something to hide.

- **Combination resumes**, also known as *creative resumes,* combine elements of chronological and functional resumes. These are the most creative and adaptable types of resumes and are the favorite choice of many teacher applicants.

    Advantages: Uses the best ideas from both styles: teaching experience, related experience, activities and distinctions, interests, skills, and educational background. Allows for a great deal of creativity.

    Disadvantages: More time-consuming to organize and difficult to read unless formatted very carefully.

What Do You Mean by "Formatting"?

Formatting is how the information is laid out on the page. There are two basic styles of formatting:

- **Block style** has a clean, sharp appearance because all the headings begin at the left margin. The information under each heading is indented about an inch and a half, giving it an "airy" look with a lot of white space.

- **Centered style** uses full margins and wider lines. This is an excellent choice if you have a great deal of information to include on a one-page resume.

"What impresses me most about a candidate's resume and application is the professional presentation and the experiences outside of education that can be of benefit in dealing with kids. Also, brag a little. As they say, if you can do it, it's not bragging. Besides, you only have a few pieces of paper to prove you should be interviewed!"
—Science chair, mentor teacher, and member of the interview committee for a rural district in Northern California

However, it's not as crisp-looking as the block style and is more difficult to read.

What Is a Customized Resume?

A customized resume is one that's targeted toward a specific teaching vacancy. For example, if you're applying for a position as a high school social studies teacher with adjunct duties as cheerleading advisor, you'd want to include your high school and college cheerleading experiences, the fact that your cheerleading team at UCLA won first place in the Western Division finals, and your stints teaching at a summer high school cheerleading camp.

If you're applying for an overseas position teaching German to American students in Munich, you'd devote a large chunk of space to your mastery of the German language, the summer you lived with a German family in Bremen, and your knowledge of the German culture.

If you're applying for a position as a high school English and drama teacher who'll be required to direct two dramatic productions each year, you'll want to emphasize your Little Theater work, your summer experience directing a traveling production of *Our Town,* and the dramas you put together for your church youth program.

Obviously, a customized resume is a smart way to market yourself when you have transferable skills or experiences that match the special requirements listed in a particular job description. Because today's word-processing technology makes it so easy to make alterations to your basic resume, there's no excuse for sending the same canned resume in response to each vacancy you are interested in. We suggest that you target each resume to the particular job. A little effort here may make the difference between making or missing the cut.

What Are the Basic Guidelines for Resume Writing?

In a nutshell:

- Use 8½ × 11 white or off-white paper, 20-pound bond or better.
- Try to avoid using the pronoun "I."
- Make all headings uniform—the same font and size.
- The font size for body text and headings should be between 10 and 12 points, except for your name, which can be in 14- to 24-point type to make it stand out.
- If your resume has two or more pages, number each page and include your name on the second page.

- Don't use a staple or paper clip.
- Don't print on both sides of the paper.
- Don't get cute with too many novelty graphics, gothic fonts, shadowed letters, or fancy borders; this is not an art project. Above all, you want your resume to be readable, so avoid any special effects that clutter it up or make it look unprofessional.
- Prepare your resume yourself using a word-processing program so that you can update or customize it on short notice.
- Use a high-quality ink-jet or laser printer if possible.

How Long Does It Take to Write a Resume?

A simple chronological resume may take as little as two hours, but a functional or combination resume takes from five to 15 hours. You don't sit down over a cup of coffee and write your resume like you would a personal letter. It takes a great deal of thought, information gathering, creative writing, and editing. Many resume-writing experts even suggest that you work on it an hour or so at a time and then come back to it the next day. (You can see why professional resume writers don't come cheap.)

What Makes a Resume Unacceptable?

A resume that has any of these problems is unacceptable:

- Handwritten
- Typos or misspelled words
- Long, rambling sentences
- Lack of organization
- Use of the pronoun "I"
- A "crowded" look with little white space
- Poor print quality
- Handwritten corrections
- A shopworn look (bent corners, creases, smudges, or stains)

A member of an interview committee for a suburban district in Michigan was asked what impressed him most about a resume or application, and he said "Brevity—the ability to get to the point."

What Makes a Resume Outstanding?

According to our research, these are the qualities school-district personnel directors hope to see:

- Brief and concise
- Easy to read
- No more than three to five headings
- Tasteful and moderate use of font sizes, italics, boldface print, underlining, and capital letters
- Uniform margins, preferably no smaller than an inch on all sides
- A crisp, clean, professional look
- Power verbs and teaching-specific keywords
- No amateurish gimmicks
- Skills, talents, and abilities that are transferable to the classroom
- *No typos!*
- *No misspelled words!*

We've emphasized the last two qualities because we heard them repeatedly during our research. We can't stress them enough! The personnel people who do the initial screening of applications and resumes expect perfection; they often feel that teachers, above all, should be able to spell and avoid typographical errors. So be warned: There's practically no room for error here.

Recently, a company called Office Team surveyed executives of companies nationwide and asked how they felt about these same resume flaws. The results of the survey show that standards in the business world are not very different from standards in the educational arena:

- The general attitude is "Two strikes and you're out," meaning that any combination of two typos or misspelled words disqualifies the candidate from further consideration.
- Nearly 45 percent of the executives polled said it takes only *one* of these errors to eliminate the candidate from the running!

A recent poll of professional resume writers and career counselors from the Career Masters Institute also placed typos at the top of the list of cardinal resume sins.

Obviously, it's imperative that you avoid these errors, and this is what we recommend to ensure a flawless resume:

- Run a spell check. But remember that the spell check won't catch it if you use the wrong word, such as using the verb "affect" when you meant the noun "effect."
- Use a dictionary to look up the spelling of *any* word in doubt.
- Give copies of your resume to several peers for them to review and edit.
- Read your resume backwards, beginning with the last word at the bottom of the page and ending at the top. This is a clever trick that helps you catch typos and misspelled words that you often miss when reading normally, because it forces you to see only one word at a time. (Try finding the mistake in *this* sentence by reading it backwords, and you'll see what we mean.)

What Are "Power" Verbs and Keywords?

Power verbs are what bring a resume to life. A power verb reveals an impressive ability or character trait in a single word and keeps your resume from being lifeless and repetitive. Use them liberally throughout your resume. Here are some examples:

Achieved	Demonstrated	Guided
Acquired	Designed	Handled
Administered	Developed	Helped
Advocated	Devised	Implemented
Analyzed	Directed	Improved
Assessed	Drafted	Increased
Attained	Encouraged	Influenced
Authored	Enriched	Initiated
Chaired	Established	Installed
Coached	Evaluated	Instructed
Communicated	Exceeded	Interacted
Completed	Executed	Interviewed
Composed	Expanded	Introduced
Conceived	Expedited	Judged
Conducted	Facilitated	Led
Coordinated	Formulated	Maintained
Created	Founded	Managed
Delegated	Generated	Mentored

- Moderated
- Molded
- Motivated
- Negotiated
- Operated
- Organized
- Originated
- Perfected
- Performed
- Persuaded
- Pioneered
- Planned
- Prepared

- Presented
- Presided
- Produced
- Promoted
- Proposed
- Recommended
- Reorganized
- Researched
- Resolved
- Revamped
- Revitalized
- Scheduled
- Selected

- Solicited
- Solved
- Spearheaded
- Supervised
- Supported
- Taught
- Tested
- Trained
- Troubleshot
- Tutored
- Updated
- Utilized
- Wrote

Keywords (also known as buzzwords) are nouns that are used most often to describe the skills and experience that pertain to a particular profession. They demonstrate that you understand and have experience in the profession. Keywords are particularly important if you are applying to a large school corporation that might scan your resume into an electronic database of resumes. The more appropriate keywords your resume contains, the more likely it is that your resume will come up when the database is searched for candidates that match the hiring criteria. Here are some examples of education keywords, from *Expert Resumes for Teachers and Educators:*

- Accreditation
- Administration
- Athletics/coaching
- Classroom teaching
- Course design
- Instructional media
- Instrumental music
- Manipulatives
- Peer counseling
- Research
- Scholastic standards
- Standardized testing

- Student services
- Student teaching
- Textbook review

Should I List My References on My Resume?

The consensus of opinion is that you should not, for several reasons:

- You don't want to unnecessarily subject your references to constant telephone calls.
- It takes up too much valuable space.
- Employers already know you have a list of references or letters of reference. They will request a copy if they're seriously interested in you.

By the way, the jury seems to be out on whether to include this phrase at the bottom of your resume:

References available upon request.

Many feel it is a waste of space because employers already know this. Others might feel that because references are so important in the education field, you should let the school know that you have them and are ready to provide them.

Sample Resumes

Now that you have a handle on the basics, here is a collection of well-written sample resumes that demonstrate these basics in a variety of styles. Choose the one that comes closest to your qualifications, interests, specializations, and experiences, and then build from there, capitalizing on your own strengths and abilities.

RHONDA L. LeCOMPTE
202 Arborway
Jamaica Plain, MA 02130

Telephone: (617) 555-3571

E-mail: RLecompte@aol.com

CREDENTIALS:

- Certified to Teach Bilingual Education (K-8)
- Certified to Teach Special Education
- Certified to Teach Elementary Education (K-8)

EDUCATION:

M.A. Applied Linguistics (Bilingual, ESL Education)   **Summa Cum Laude, 1999**
— University of Massachusetts, Boston, Massachusetts

B.S. Special Education   **Magna Cum Laude, 1990**
Dual Major: Special Education, Mental Retardation & Elementary Education
Concentration: Psychology
— University of Maine at Farmington   1986-1990
— Université du Maine, LeMans, France   Spring Semester 1987
— University of Maine, Orono   1985-1986

Academic Awards / Achievements:
— Certificates of Award for Highest GPA in MR Major (1988, Spring)   UMF
  & Outstanding Academic Achievement (1988, Spring)
— Alpha Lambda Delta / National Scholastic Honor Society for Freshmen UMO
— Selected (1 of 3 Students at the University) to participate in a
  Special Education Delegation to the People's Republic of China   UMF

QUALIFICATIONS:

- Bilingual (English & Spanish).
- Experience in one-on-one tutoring and group instruction of ESL.
- Experienced in client assistance working with the mentally retarded - teaching living skills to adolescents and adults.
- Designed and implemented a new program for teaching life skills which is currently successfully being used in a high school setting.
- Experienced in conceptualization, consultation, and presentation of varied-level educational workshops/conferences.
- Serve as a teaching consultant to other teachers involved in the process of integrating students into other programs and classes.
- Published in *Racenicity: The Whitewashing of Ethnicity* by Pepi Leistyna (Chapter 6) / Publisher: Roman & Littlefield (forthcoming)

(Continued on Page Two)

Figure 3.1: This resume for a bilingual/special/elementary teacher was very effective in generating interviews for positions in highly competitive school districts. (Resume writer: Rolande LaPointe, Lewiston, ME)

Rhonda L. LeCompte   Curriculum Vitae (Page Two)

TEACHING EXPERIENCE:

Bi-Lingual (Spanish) Special Education Teacher   **Fall 1999-Present**
Cambridge High School (Cambridge, Massachusetts)
— Designed, implemented, and administer new Life Skills Program
— Mentor to several high school students

Spanish Instructor   **Summer 1998**
UMASS, Boston, Massachusetts / Veteran's Upward Bound Program

Substitute Teacher   **1996-1999**
Boston School System (Boston, Massachusetts)

ESL Instructor   **1996-1998**
Cambridge Center for Adult Education (Cambridge, Massachusetts)

Bilingual Special Education Teacher   **1995-1996**
Thomas Jefferson Elementary School (Boston, Massachusetts)
— K-3 Self-contained language room

Peace Corps Volunteer (Cuenca, Ecuador)   **1993-1995**
Special Education Teacher Consultant
Instituto Psicopedagogico Agustin Cueva Tamariz (Cuenca, Ecuador)
— Total program conducted in the Spanish language, grades K-6.
— Consulted with multiple teachers, classrooms, and students.
— Implemented/presented individual and classroom consultation programs
  for teachers.
— Demonstrated planning/presentation of lessons through model teaching.

Special Education Teacher (Behaviorally Impaired)   **1990-1993**
Montello Jr. High School (Lewiston, Maine)
— Self-contained classroom for 7th and 8th grade students.
— Supervised 1-2 Education Techs.
— Outstanding Teacher Award (1992-1993), Lewiston Teacher's Association.

ANNE C. ELLIS

210 Candlewood Court, Lacey, Washington 98509
ellisedu@earthlink.com   378-245-1256

OBJECTIVE

A position as an Elementary School Teacher that will utilize strong teaching abilities to create a nurturing, motivational, and stimulating learning environment to help children achieve their potential.

PROFILE

- Highly motivated, enthusiastic, and dedicated educator who wants all children to be successful learners.
- "Believe in the impossible"; continually research educational programs and procedures to benefit students.
- Committed to creating a classroom atmosphere that is stimulating and encouraging to students.
- Demonstrated ability to consistently individualize instruction, based on student's needs and interests.
- Exceptional ability to establish cooperative, professional relationships with parents, staff, and administration.

EDUCATION

B.S. in Elementary Education, Troy State University, Troy, Alabama   2000
- Summa Cum Laude — President's Honor List — Kappa Delta Phi
- National Collegiate Education Award Winner
- Who's Who Among Students in American Universities and Colleges
- Participated in the Test for Teaching Knowledge field project, 2000
A.A. in Arts and Sciences, Pierce College, Tacoma, Washington   1995

CREDENTIALS

Elementary Education: 1-6:   Alabama License (Pending) — Washington License (Pending)

STUDENT TEACHING

Student Teacher, Harrand Creek Elementary School, Dothan, Alabama   Fall 2000
- Completed 200 hours hands-on teaching; resulting in a total of 488 hours experience in a first grade classroom. Utilized children's literature to teach and reinforce reading, writing, grammar, and phonics. Coordinated and taught math lessons and activities. Collaborated with teacher in planning, preparing, and organizing thematic units. Observed the use of teaching techniques to meet the needs of visual, kinesthetic, and auditory learners for all subject areas. Assisted in the quarterly grading.
Classroom Intern, Harrand Creek Elementary School, Dothan, Alabama (60 hours)
2nd Grade, Reading, Clover Park Elementary School, Dothan, Alabama
4th Grade, Reading, Science, Social Studies, Headland Elementary School, Dothan, Alabama
4th Grade, Math, EastGate Elementary School, Dothan, Alabama
5th Grade, Art & Social Studies, EastGate Middle School, Ozark, Alabama
1st Grade, Reading Tutor for student at-risk program, Troy State University, Alabama

RELATED EXPERIENCE

Director, Kinder-Care Learning Center, Lacey, Washington   1993 to 1995
Oversaw day-to-day operations of child care center for 65 children. Ensured all local, state, and federal rules and regulations were adhered to.

AFFILIATIONS

Member, National Council for Exceptional Children
Leader, Girl Scouts of America

Figure 3.2: This resume for a newly qualified teacher makes a strong visual impression through the use of unusual fonts and a striking graphic. (Resume writer: Teresa L. Pearson, Rucker, AL)

LINDA QUI

1502 Lin Grove Blvd. #615 — Houston, TX 77087 — (713) 555-5555

OBJECTIVE: A full-time elementary school teaching position

HIGHLIGHTS OF QUALIFICATIONS:

- More than 8 years of successful work experience in an academic environment
- Bachelor of Fine Arts degree and currently working toward Master's degree in Education
- Experience working with preschool and elementary-age children
- Exceptionally creative with proven organizational, planning, and leadership skills

RELEVANT EXPERIENCE:

Teaching

KILLEEN INDEPENDENT SCHOOL DISTRICT - Killeen, IA
Student Teacher's Assistant for summer art program *(Kindergarten through first grade)*

FIRST BAPTIST CHURCH - Southtown, TX
Vacation Bible School and Sunday School Teacher *(Preschool through first grade)*

UNIVERSITY OF RICHMOND, THE HONORS COLLEGE - Richmond, TX
Academic Advisor, Orientation Advisor, and Retreat Counselor for students of the Honors College

Planning and Organization

UNIVERSITY OF RICHMOND, THE HONORS COLLEGE - Richmond, TX
Coordinator – "Little Wrangler Day" in cooperation with the Richmond Independent School District. During this successful event, over 3000 elementary school students observed cultural exhibits.

Chairman - University of Richmond Annual Fiesta Association
(A student-run festival event benefiting community scholarship programs)
- Advised and oversaw all event committees.
- Created and produced the Annual Fiesta Policy Manual and the Annual Fiesta Gazette.
- Created recruitment programs and served as Scholarship Coordinator and Director of Community Relations.
- Held overall responsibility for event's $126,000 budget.

EMPLOYMENT HISTORY:

UNIVERSITY OF RICHMOND, THE HONORS COLLEGE - Richmond, TX	
Administrative Assistant	1996 to Present
Chairman - Annual Fiesta Association	1995 to 1996
Assistant to the Scholarship Coordinator	1992 to 1994
UNIVERSITY OF KILLEEN - Killeen, IA	
Residential Clerk	1992
THE PHOTOGRAPHERS - Stafford, TX	
Office Assistant	1988 to 1992

Figure 3.3: Without a teaching certificate, this individual used a functional style to show her experience with young children and was successful in landing a position with the school district's Alternative Certification Program. (Resume writer: Kelley Smith, Sugar Land, TX)

Linda Qui — Page 2

EDUCATION:

UNIVERSITY OF RICHMOND - Richmond, TX
Bachelor of Fine Arts (1997)
GPA 3.4 / Graduated with membership in The Honors College
*Currently enrolled in coursework toward **M.Ed. in Educational Psychology***

Awards:

- Outstanding Senior Service Award
- Ambud of the Year
- Ambassador of the Year
- Areté Award

MEMBERSHIPS & CERTIFICATIONS:

- University of Richmond Alumni Association, *Young Alumni Board of Directors*
- Annual Fiesta Association, *Chairman*
- Honors College Student Governing Board
- Honors College Advisory Board
- Honors Advocates, *Coordinator*
- Richmond Livestock Show and Rodeo Committee
- Certified Alcohol Intervention Trainer

Excellent references and letters of recommendation available

Shayla Miller

3211 Pine Grove Lane • Richmond, Virginia 23219
804-555-9278 • smiller02@richmond.com

OBJECTIVE

To obtain a teaching position in Elementary Education, K–6

SUMMARY OF QUALIFICATIONS

- Initiate programs to foster inclusivity and respect among students.
- Collaborate with other educators to create new learning experiences for students.
- Use creativity and the arts to promote enjoyment of learning.
- Gear teaching style to include students with various abilities and functional levels.

PROFESSIONAL EXPERIENCE

9/2004–present
Pine Grove Elementary School, Richmond School District, Richmond, Virginia
Teacher, Grade 3, Leave Replacement Position

- Plan and implement Virginia Standards in all subject areas.
- Encourage extra reading by developing extensive classroom library.
- Utilize manipulatives in mathematics and science for hands-on understanding.
- Participate in district's math curriculum writing team.
- Direct third grade Drama Club.
- Team-teach with fourth grade teacher for combined-group reading lessons.
- Participate in PTA.
- Initiated and continue weekly inclusion of students from Boces special education class.

12/2003–6/2004
Madison Central School District, Madison, Virginia
Substitute Teacher, Grades K–6

- Managed classroom as appropriate to each grade level.
- Implemented lesson plans and added personal expertise to classroom activities.

STUDENT TEACHING EXPERIENCE

9/2003–12/2003
Centerton Elementary School, Madison, Virginia
Student Teacher, Grade 3 and Kindergarten

- Enacted strategic planning procedures to facilitate students' meaningful engagement with curriculum.
- Developed personal teaching approach centered on active engagement and cooperative learning.
- Created instructional materials and strategies consistent with students' learning and behavioral needs.
- Evaluated and analyzed students with special needs; attended instructional support meetings.

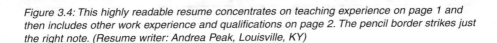

Figure 3.4: This highly readable resume concentrates on teaching experience on page 1 and then includes other work experience and qualifications on page 2. The pencil border strikes just the right note. (Resume writer: Andrea Peak, Louisville, KY)

Shayla Miller Resume – page 2

ADDITIONAL WORK EXPERIENCE

6/1998–2/2002
Lazarus, Columbus, Ohio
Sales Manager

- Responsible for all aspects of daily operation: recruitment, training of personnel, store presentation, inventory control, scheduling, and customer relations.
- Assumed New Store Coordinator position with additional responsibilities of organizing and opening of all new stores in Tri-State area, including recruitment, staffing, employee development, receiving, and store setup.

ARTISTIC BACKGROUND

- Classically trained in voice and piano.
- Various recitals in Chicago area; performed with Chicago Opera Company and various regional and national opera companies.
- Fifteen years of theatrical training: directing, acting, cabaret, and improvisation.

COMPUTER SKILLS

- Microsoft Word
- Microsoft Excel
- Internet browser and e-mail applications

EDUCATION AND CERTIFICATION

Richmond University, Richmond, Virginia
- *Master of Science in Elementary Education*, 12/2003
  GPA: 3.8/4.0
- *Certification Program of Reading*, in process

Ashland University, Ashland, Ohio
- *Bachelor of Fine Arts*, 5/2002
  Major in Opera Performance

Virginia State Provisional Certification, Grades K–6, 5/2004

Virginia State Provisional Certification, Grades K–12, Music, 5/2004

Family Math Training Workshop, 10/2003

Identification and Reporting of Child Abuse and Maltreatment, 3/2003

Sarah Elizabeth Keane

123 Winter Tree Drive • Litchfield, CT 06759-3324
860-555-5555 • sekeane@aol.com

STUDENT-FOCUSED FAMILY AND CONSUMER SCIENCE TEACHER
OFFERING HANDS-ON EXPERIENCE

- *Child Development*
- *Parenting*
- *Foods /Nutrition*
- *Life Skills*
- *Interior Design*
- *Budgeting*
- *Menu Planning*
- *Sewing*

PROFILE

📖 *Classroom Instruction*—Enthusiastic, committed educator with innate ability to understand and motivate students. Continuously strive to build self-esteem and encourage understanding of cultural diversity, gender differences, physical limitations, and learning ability. Committed to creating a classroom atmosphere that is stimulating and encouraging. Safety conscious and observant of student behavior and actions. Demonstrated ability to individualize instruction.

📖 *Education Relationships*—Team player adept at establishing and fostering cooperative professional relationships with parents and administration. Diplomatic approach to parent-teacher relationships. Actively solicit and encourage parents' participation to ensure student progress.

📖 *Personal Attributes*—Outstanding interpersonal skills, having dealt with a broad diversity of education professionals, students, and parents. Easily establish rapport and trust. Highly motivated to expand knowledge and skills. Enjoy keeping current with new developments and trends in education. Well-organized and adept at multitasking and prioritizing. Powerful communication skills, verbal and written. Computer skills include Word, Excel, PowerPoint, Publisher, and Internet.

"Sarah is a quality teacher in every sense of the word and would add a high degree of improvement to any facility. She has worked with difficult students and has not only managed to control and educate them, but also gain their respect."

Stanley Ward, *Director*
Prospect Continuing Education

"Her forte is her ability to connect with children and parents alike. She is able to establish a working relationship with children of all identities. She is reliable, trustworthy...and is valued and respected by her students, co-workers, administration and our community."

April Carr, *Special Education Teacher*
Sanswood Elementary School

"She has the ability to encourage academic growth in students while enhancing their self esteem. Her knowledge, ability to teach, compassion, and eagerness to motivate students is inspiring."

Fred Turner, *Teacher*
Conard High School

"(Sarah) is astute in her recognition of and awareness of individual student needs. She uses consulting time effectively and is creative in her approach to problem solving. Sarah is a great team player. She is a good listener and effectively offers input in group collaboration."

Patrick Shatner, MSW, *School Social Worker*
Conard High School

EDUCATION

WESTERN CONNECTICUT STATE UNIVERSITY, Danbury, CT
Currently pursuing coursework towards a Master of Science in School Counseling (2000 to Present)

UNIVERSITY OF BRIDGEPORT, Bridgeport, CT
Master of Science—Education (1992)
Certification—Provisional Educator Certificate Pre K–8
Consumer and Family Science K–12 (3.8 GPA)

UNIVERSITY OF CONNECTICUT, Storrs, CT
Bachelor of Science—Human Development and Family Relations

Figure 3.5: A very strong profile, supplemented by exceptional testimonials, creates a block-buster opening for this resume. Extensive teaching experience is detailed on page 2. (Resume writer: Ross Primack, Wethersfield, CT)

Sarah Elizabeth Keane   **Page Two**

CAREER HISTORY

RAFFIN MIDDLE SCHOOL   Hartford, CT   2003 to Present
Grade 7 Reading Teacher

- ❑ Coordinate efforts with colleagues to develop and implement reading strategies.
- ❑ Provide students with comprehensive preparation for Connecticut Mastery Tests.
- ❑ Develop and modify lesson plans. Administer tests and grade student papers.
- ❑ Create visually appealing and informative bulletin boards.
- ❑ Review student records and prepare PPTs.
- ❑ Process paperwork from the Department of Children and Family Services.

HARPER ELEMENTARY SCHOOL   Woodbury, CT   1998 to 2003
Grade 5 Teacher

- ❑ Developed, taught, modified, and assessed lessons for class of 22 students.
- ❑ Implemented structured behavior modification plans.
- ❑ Conducted semiannual conferences with parents.
- ❑ Coordinated all facets of field trip planning, including reservations, fundraising, and chaperoning.
- ❑ Served as 5th grade SAT team representative to address and develop strategies for special needs students.
- ❑ Represented 5th grade on faculty council. Met monthly with colleagues to address issues and concerns. Disseminated issues for discussion with principal.

CONARD HIGH SCHOOL   West Hartford, CT   1997 to 1998
Child Development Teacher

- ❑ Taught child development unit to high school students.
- ❑ Coordinated efforts with Naugatuck Valley Community College to enable participants of high school class to receive college credit for completed coursework.

PROSPECT ADULT EDUCATION   Prospect, CT   1994 to 1995
Part-Time Facilitator/Instructor

- ❑ Facilitated adult education programs on topics including cooking and custom decorating.

SANSWOOD ELEMENTARY SCHOOL   Woodbury, CT   1992 to 1998
Title 1 Teacher

- ❑ Teamed with classroom teachers to develop and implement remedial and enrichment curriculum for grades K–5.
- ❑ Assisted with all facets of student evaluations.
- ❑ Chaperoned field trips.

PROFESSIONAL DEVELOPMENT

- *Meeting Individual Student Needs*
- *Health Curriculum K–12*

- *Student Portfolio Assessment*
- *Health Curriculum Committee*

- *Writing Project (Grade 5)*
- *Classroom Management*

RICHARD OLSON
3605 North 86th Street
Superior, Wisconsin 54880
(715) 555-1692 or olson@cc.com

OBJECTIVE:

Elementary or Middle School Social Studies Teacher

HIGHLIGHTS OF QUALIFICATIONS:

- Numerous practica experiences in local schools.
- Total commitment to students, district, school, and community.
- Highly effective communicator.
- Compassionate and sensitive to needs and emotions of children.
- 11 years of experience coaching boys' baseball. Expertise in both on-field coaching and off-field administration of game.
- Committed to personal lifelong learning as well as offering quality education to children.

LICENSE:

Wisconsin teaching license. Certified to teach elementary education and Social Studies Grades 7–9.

EDUCATION:

University of Wisconsin—Superior (UWS)
BS, Elementary Education with **Social Studies** minor, May 2004.
GPA: 3.79. Involved in Future Teachers Association.

AWARDS:

UWS, Dean's List of Academic Achievement, 2002–2003; Fairbrother Academic Scholarship, 2003–2004; Lakehead Pipeline Company, Incorporated, Academic Scholarship, Spring 2003; Maurice Brown Academic Scholarship, 2002–2003; and UWS Foundation Academic Scholarship, 2001–2002.

PRACTICA:

Social Studies Methods, Lester Park Middle School, Duluth, MN, Spring 2003
Language Arts Methods, St. James Elementary School, Superior, WI, Fall 2002
Reading Methods, St. James Elementary School, Superior, WI, Fall 2002
Physical Education Methods, Cooer Elementary School, Superior, WI, Spring 2002

COACHING:

Baseball, Boys Legion (ages 16–18), Great Falls, MI, Youth Baseball Association, 1991–1997
Baseball, Boys Senior Little League (ages 13–15), Great Falls, MI, Youth Baseball Association, 1987–1990
- American Legion Baseball Program experienced phenomenal growth during tenure. Player enrollment increased to such an extent as to necessitate need for Junior Varsity Club. Promoted Legion baseball in community, raising awareness of it to higher level.
- Assisted several players to continue playing in college through on-site coaching and personal contacts with college coaches.
- Effectively assisted American Legion Club members in securing funds for program allowing for expenditures to be used in more beneficial manner.
- Work, tireless commitment, and knowledge of game earned me position with Atlanta Braves as Associate Scout.

Figure 3.6: A lot of information is packed into this resume for a newly qualified teacher. It was important to include coaching and employment activities that gave him lots of experience working with children. (Resume writer: Linda Wunner)

Richard Olson

EMPLOYMENT:

School District of Superior, WI
Intern, January–June 2004
Interning in 6th grade classroom at Great Falls Elementary School. Assume responsibilities of regular classroom teacher: recording attendance, teaching all subjects, administering and correcting tests, and exercising needed discipline. Already employed as substitute teacher where I have interacted with other teachers and school employees in various capacities.

- Coordinated 6th grade fundraiser that raised more than $2,000.
- Co-director of district-wide spelling bee that involved communications with district principals and teachers.
- Participated in after-school "Math Olympiad" program, a supplemental math activity for students seeking additional challenges.
- Assisted in school's participation in nationwide oration and writing contests.

University of Wisconsin–Superior
Game Management, 2001–Present
Administer smooth, effective execution of all sports programs. Welcome visiting teams and provide necessary assistance. Secure and supervise workers for events.

- Key player in significantly improving UWS's hospitality image through hard work, effective planning, and personable communication.
- Successfully assisted in staffing 2004 NCAA Division III Men's Hockey National Finals Tournament.

VISTA (Volunteers in Service to America), Superior, WI
Summer Associate, May–August 2003
Strived to improve literacy of at-risk students. Created and learned about several literacy assessment tools used to select appropriate literacy experiences and assessed impact of total summer school experience on students. Served as resource person for paraprofessionals and helped prepare resource materials for other tutors.

- Effectively tutored 4 primary grade students in reading and writing daily.
- Developed evaluation tools, including rubrics, surveys, and other assessments, that were used as before-and-after measures for program.
- In conjunction with other summer associates, developed recruitment and training plan.

City of Great Falls Parks Department, Great Falls, MI
Park Maintenance Worker, Summers 1997–2001
Resurrected and maintained beauty of 22-acre city baseball complex.

Sheridan Lanes, Great Falls, MI
Assistant Manager, 1990–2001
Successfully ensured customer satisfaction for business by establishing rapport and communication. Managed leagues and maintained facility.

- Reestablished youth bowling leagues.
- Successfully managed/hosted annual tournaments.
- Remained loyal during several ownership changes.

THOMAS B. KLEIN

89 Kensington Road • Manahawkin, NJ 08050 • 609-612-8985 • tbklein@verion.net

— High-School English Teacher for Your Most Challenging Students —
— Football Coach —

SUMMARY

Spirited, optimistic education professional with an excellent reputation for spurring dramatic improvements in the classroom performance, behavior, and attitude of lower-track high-school students deemed "unteachable." Able to gain the trust and respect of youngsters and convey confidence in their abilities. Successful in using innovative, unconventional approaches to engage students' interest, strengthen reading and writing skills, develop an appreciation for literature, and achieve high passing rates on standardized proficiency tests. Initiator and manager of a unique, highly effective in-school suspension program. Extensive coaching background.

SKILLS AND ACCOMPLISHMENTS

Classroom Teaching
- Consistently sought the challenge of teaching and inspiring lower-track high-school students.
- Achieved outstanding success in strengthening their reading and writing abilities, building life skills, and motivating them to consider job / career goals; 25% of students pursued higher education.
- Encouraged students to become active classroom participants and join in the decision-making process.
- Attained an HSPT passing percentage in the upper 80% range among students who had previously failed.
- Effectively used comic books and other unconventional resources to build grammar and punctuation skills.
- Organized spirited debates on controversial topics.
- Sparked students' interest in literature through role playing and lively discussions.
- Arranged for monthly guest speakers to address career topics.

Behavior Management / Counseling
- Achieved one of the lowest rates of discipline problems in the school.
- Created a fun, free-spirited environment in which students adhered to stated rules of conduct.
- Worked closely with parents to reinforce behavior management.
- Developed trusting relationships with students and frequently served as a sounding board for problems.
- Helped students develop a better outlook and a solution-oriented approach to dealing with challenges.

Program Development and Management
- Initiated the introduction of a learning-based in-school suspension program to deal with a high rate of daily suspensions; later instituted the program at a middle school based on outstanding results.
- Coordinated each student's assignments with classroom teacher and provided one-on-one instruction in all subject areas. For the first time in the school's history, required suspended students to perform schoolwork.

Coaching
- Coached several undefeated football teams, including one that went on to win the state championship.
- Helped sharpen the skills of many players who later played college football.
- Oversaw the entire football program for 6 Pop Warner teams; interacted with local school coaches to integrate their philosophies into the program, so players are well-prepared for high school football.

PROFESSIONAL EXPERIENCE

Pomeranz High School, Newark, NJ:
Director of In-School Suspension Program / Teacher (2000–Present)
English Teacher, Grades 9–12 (1980–2000)
Assistant Football Coach (1986–1990) / Head Football Coach (1990–1992) / Head Baseball Coach (1992)
Assistant Coach, Football / Baseball / Wrestling (1990–1991)

COMMUNITY SERVICE / AWARDS

Football Commissioner, Angels Athletic Association / Pop Warner Football, Manahawkin, NJ (1998–Present)
Football Coach, Pop Warner Football, Manahawkin / Newark, NJ (1985–1998)
Community Service Award, Kaitland County Chamber of Commerce (2003)

CERTIFICATION / EDUCATION

Certification as Teacher of High School English, State of New Jersey
B.A., English / Communications, 1980 • Rutgers University, New Brunswick, NJ
Graduate Credits in Curriculum and Administration • Monmouth University, W. Long Branch, NJ

Figure 3.7: This high school teacher wants to take on a school's "most challenging students," and the functional Skills and Accomplishments list effectively highlights his ability to do so. (Resume writer: Rhoda Kopy, Toms River, NJ)

TONY C. RICHARDSON

328 Shattauck Avenue
Palm Bay, FL 32907
(321) 725-5135

PURSUING A POSITION IN TEACHING

Certifications and Endorsements: K-12 Physical Education, Health, and Science 6-12

SUMMARY OF QUALIFICATIONS

Professional committed to achieving favorable results in education through a positive impact on the children of today and the future. Recognized leader for professional, academic, and community contributions. Experience and academic training include:

- Teaching Practices
- Management Info. Systems
- Personnel Evaluations
- Future Planning
- Classroom Evaluation

- Curriculum Inquiry
- Violence in Schools
- Time Management
- Leadership
- Athletic Coaching

- Measurement & Evaluation
- Educational Systems
- Classroom Dynamics
- Curriculum Evaluation
- Community Relations

EDUCATION

M.S. in Educational Leadership, Florida State University — 12/99; GPA: 3.88
B.S. in Human Performance Dynamics; Concentration in Teaching K-12, University of South Florida — 12/96; GPA: 3.68

RELEVANT EXPERIENCE & SKILLS

Curriculum Development / Inquiry
- Developed curriculum for student teaching projects for health and social sciences.
- Researched the effectiveness of utilizing different styles of tests as assessments of learning.
- Wrote paper on preparing teachers for dealing with issues on mainstreaming, classroom behavior, perceived ability to teach special needs, classroom management, and academic development of the special needs child.

Educational Measurement
- Examined various assessment methods, tools, techniques, processes, and procedures in evaluating student performance for Measurement and Evaluation in Education.
- Completed a project on student learning styles to ascertain the prevalence of oral and visual learners and their related study habits.

Teaching / Presentation
- Developed strong presentation and teaching style by utilizing a variety of educational tools including games, team-building exercises, use of videos, lectures, and alternative activities.
- Skilled speaker, comfortable in presenting to groups as a manager and community volunteer.

VOLUNTEER / EMPLOYMENT EXPERIENCE

Volunteer
- Student Teacher, University High School, Orlando, FL — 1999 to 2000
- Coach, Volunteer, Youth Football League of Sanford, FL — 1996 to Present
- Den Leader, Boy Scouts of America, Orlando, FL — 1995 to Present
- Coach, Volunteer, Youth of America, Orlando, FL — 1994 to 1997
- Park Supervisor, Seminole County Recreation Department, Orlando, FL — 1990 to 1993

Employment
- Operations Manager, B.J.'s Wholesale Warehouse, Merritt Island, FL — 1997 to Present
- Department Supervisor, B.J.'s Wholesale Warehouse, Merritt Island, FL — 1994 to 1997
- Sales Associate, B.J.'s Wholesale Warehouse, Merritt Island, FL — 1993 to 1994

Figure 3.8: With no teaching experience but lots of pertinent volunteer and coaching activities, this individual highlighted his relevant experience and skills to add weight to his qualifications. (Resume writer: Laura DeCarlo, Melbourne, FL)

Cecilia M. Diaz
55 Magnolia Lane, Oakland, NJ 07436
201-405-5555 ▪ cmdiaz@net.com

Career Target

Middle School Science Teacher in a child-centered school district.

Summary
- ☑ Highly motivated, energetic educator with 15 years of middle school teaching experience.
- ☑ Strong track record of fostering student curiosity, creativity, and enhanced learning.
- ☑ Enthusiastic, warm, and caring professional, sensitive to students' specialized and changing needs.
- ☑ Demonstrated ability to deliver individualized instruction, appropriate to each student's abilities.
- ☑ Ability to act as liaison, harmoniously and effectively, between parents, school, and community.

Key Skill Areas

Instructional Strategies
- Designed and developed integrated, thematic physical science curriculum for middle school students, aligned to meet core content and state standards.
- Use cross-curriculum, cooperative learning, motivational environment, team planning, and "real-world" examples to stimulate learning and learner retention.

Learning Styles
- Achieve educational goals by incorporating learning modality principles into all instruction. First special-service teacher incorporated into an inclusion class.
- Emphasize an active learning environment, high student expectations, and individualized instruction in a student-centered, heterogeneous classroom.

Educational Technology
- Championed innovative physical science programs and activities utilizing instructional media to enhance the scope and quality of education.
- Accomplished in the use of hands-on materials, manipulatives, and technology (electron microscopes, research on the Internet, video cameras, software).

Leadership
- Pioneered "Scientists in the Classroom" Program, partnering with local companies to provide scientific demonstrations and Q&A sessions.
- Selected as judge for state-run program, "21st Century Science"—3 years.

Student / Parent Relations
- Fostered parent involvement through regular communication (telephone calls or notes daily) and invitations to participate in classroom activities and events.
- Natural gift for getting young students excited about learning.

Certifications and Education

New Jersey Permanent Certification K–8 Elementary
New Jersey Permanent Certification K–12 English

1995 M.Ed., Stockton State College, Stockton, NJ
1983 B.S., Elementary Education & English, Clemson University, Clemson, SC

Continuing Education:
2001 Meteorology Course, Union College, School of Meteorology
1998 Certificate, Computer Educator, Passaic County College, Passaic, NJ
1996 Materials Science Conference, sponsored by Rutgers University
1992 Cooperative Learning, Conference on Scientific Curriculum

Computer Skills

Macintosh PCs	MS Word	MS Works	Netscape Navigator
ClarisWorks	MacGrade	Internet	E-mail

Figure 3.9: This two-page resume devotes as much attention to activities leadership as it does to teaching descriptions. It also uses a broad Key Skill Areas section to emphasize relevant achievements. (Resume writer: Susan Guarneri, Lawrenceville, NJ)

Cecilia M. Diaz
201-405-5555 • Page 2

Experience

1989–present   **Morris County Middle School,** Morristown, NJ
Science Teacher—8th Grade
- Teach Chemistry, Physics, Geology, and Meteorology as well as enrichment classes for 3 classes daily, with up to 30 students per class, utilizing curriculum compacting and tiered instruction with 5 tiered teams in a block-scheduling system.
- Designed self-learning and small-group cooperative learning activities as well as hands-on science activities such as the Cliffton House archeological excavation.

2003   **Central State Middle School,** Harrison, NJ
Substitute Teacher—Physical Science

1988–1989   **Oakland Township School District,** Oakland, NJ
Substitute Teacher—K–12, primarily 6th Grade

1984–1988   **Tiny Tots Pre-school,** Rahwah, NJ
Kindergarten Teacher / Director
- Full administrative, staffing, and budgeting responsibility for this mini-school within the district, with 13 teachers, aides, cook, and school bus driver, in addition to duties as kindergarten teacher.

Activities

1989–2001   **Advisor, MCMS Newspaper: The Tiger Ledger**
- Provided proactive leadership for this student-run newspaper. Introduced students to assignments as cartoonists, reporters, photographers, proofreaders, and editors.
- Collaborated with Morristown News to meet quarterly production deadlines. Upgraded original cut-and-paste layout to computer layout. Forged parent partnerships for fundraising activities.

1989–2000   **Advisor, MCMS Video Imaging Program Production**
- Led creative team of student volunteers in the design, editing, and production of an annual 8th grade video production, a reprise of their 8th grade year, which was shown to parents, faculty, administration, and students at the end of the school year.
- Spearheaded successful fundraising campaign that raised $10K within one year for multimedia equipment. Spun-off to become the MCMS TV Studio, a fully functioning studio with a network of TV monitors installed in every classroom.

1989–1995   **Advisor, MCMS Yearbook: The Tiger**
- Oversaw this student-run production by 7th and 8th graders, culminating in a hardcover yearbook. Students learned photography, layout, cropping, editing, and the entire production process. Raised funds to support this annual activity.

Committees & Awards

Discipline Committee—established demerit system
Mission Statement Committee—Morristown Township "Millennium Mission"
Who's Who in American Education
Board of Education Honoree—for contributions to MCMS newspaper

Professional Associations

National Education Association (NEA)
New Jersey Education Association (NJEA)
New Jersey Science Teachers Association (NJSTA)

BILL ANDERSON
265 Charlotte Street
Asheville, NC 28801

(828) 254-7893 *home*
(828) 314-7893 *cell*
banders@hometown.net

HISTORY TEACHER
North Carolina License, Social Studies 9–12

PROFILE

Proactive, uncompromising focus on improving reading, writing, and critical thinking skills. Use flexibility, resourcefulness, and organizational and interpersonal skills to assist that learning through a positive, encouraging environment.

Strengths

- Capable teacher thoroughly grounded in U.S., Middle East, World, and European History.
- Rapport-builder with parents (they think they're all alone out there), able to gain their involvement, trust, and respect in creating a participative environment.
- Adept, available, and adaptable classroom manager—combine discipline plan with effective procedures and varied lessons to attract the inattentive and enforce student accountability.
- Student motivator—can use cooperative learning and other student-directed/process learning techniques to cultivate inclusivity and build teamwork and goal-setting skills.
- Develop useful daily lesson plans and instructional resources.
- Friendly, interactive, and dependable.
- Some fluency in Spanish (can read Spanish newspaper).

"A page of history is worth a volume of logic."—Oliver Wendell Holmes

EDUCATION

B.A., History, *Magna Cum Laude,* December 2003
North Carolina University, Polk, NC

Coursework

- US. History, Medieval Europe, Politics of the Middle East, Political Science, Chinese History (Revolutionary China), Afro-American History, Human Rights & International Politics, Humanities. Dean's List every eligible semester.

Student Teaching

- Hall High School, spring and fall 2003—11th grade college prep classes in U.S. History. Despite novice ranking, selected to teach AP U.S. History class due to knowledge of material.

"I teach skill in asking questions through my skill in asking the right question...."

  - Contributions included judging senior projects, proctoring end-of-course tests, and sponsoring the fledgling Debate Club.

  - Because my co-op was on the school improvement team, was able to observe planning and goal-setting functions in the effort to meet constantly changing requirements.

  - Participated positively in parent-teacher conferences.

Honors & Affiliations

- Selected for Phi Alpha Theta History National Honor Society (high GPA and faculty recommendation).
- Selected by History Department faculty for the Mike Bolson History Scholarship as a promising student in the field of history, despite being on an education track.
- Participant, NCU History Association.
- Alpha Phi Omega National Service Fraternity—Chapter President; as Vice President of Service, initiated projects involving boys' and girls' clubs; fundraising.

Cited by department faculty for original, critical thinking....

Figure 3.10: This job seeker returned to school to earn teaching credentials after a 30-year career in manufacturing. (Resume writer: Dayna Feist, Asheville, NC)

banders@hometown.net • (828) 314–7893 *cell* • (828) 254–7893 *home*   **BILL ANDERSON**

Prior Education	**Diploma, Welding** (one-year program), 1980 WNC Technical Community College Coursework in Anthropology, Biology, Spanish, 1973 University of Massachusetts–Boston
PRIOR EXPERIENCE	BOILER OPERATOR: Culverton Textiles, Foster, NC—1981–1998 Operated steam- and electric-generating utility for largest textile mill of its kind in the world (on 10 acres), with its own waste treatment and water filtration system. A self-contained mini-city, it generated much of its own power. Member of 2-man team: managed electrical control room, maintenance, welding, machinery repair, pipefitting. ENGINEER: 100-foot Bluestocking fishing boat, Gloucester, MA—1971–1980 MACHINIST MATE: United States Navy—1967–1971 Served on the U.S.S. *Georgetown* (traveled to Mozambique Civil War; the Indian Ocean; and Havana, Cuba) and U.S.S. *Severn* (oil tanker refueling ships at sea in the Mediterranean). Trained Navy personnel (including firemen and 3rd class petty officers) to work with tools and operate equipment.
COMMUNITY REINVESTMENT	▪ Coached Roller Hockey for boys' and girls' clubs, ages 13–18, in league competition. ▪ Tutor, Afterschool Club, Salvation Army. ▪ Big Brothers/Big Sisters, 1981–1983. Mentored 7–year–old boy (gardening, movies, sports, homework).

Ann Thomas

10 Henry Street, Wycoff, New Jersey 07401
H: (201) 886-1125 — E-mail: Athomas@yahoo.com

OBJECTIVE	A position as a Middle School Mathematics Teacher where I can create an energized learning environment that focuses on individual understanding and expression.
PROFILE	Dedicated, talented, resourceful teacher skilled in building rapport and respect with students. Possess the ability to establish a creative and stimulating classroom environment. Experienced in using innovative computer software to enhance learning process. Background includes tutoring in high school, student teaching in high school and middle school, and serving as a mathematics teaching assistant at the college level.
SUMMARY OF QUALIFICATIONS	• More than 8 years of experience as a mathematics teacher and tutor. • Introduced "Studio Calculus" at Dover Institute of Technology (DIT) as a new teaching tool utilizing Maple Software. • Received award for "Outstanding Teaching Assistant" from DIT student body. • Tutored students in high school and college in mathematical principles. • Able to make subject material "come alive" for students through enthusiasm and creativity.
EDUCATION 2000-Present 1997-2000	DOVER INSTITUTE OF TECHNOLOGY, Jersey City, New Jersey Ph.D. work in Mathematics. Stanley Fellowship recipient. Master of Science in Applied Mathematics (GPA 4.0)
1994-1997	WILLIAM PATTERSON UNIVERSITY, Wayne, New Jersey Bachelor of Arts in Secondary Education (GPA 4.0), magna cum laude
EXPERIENCE 1998-Present	DOVER INSTITUTE OF TECHNOLOGY, Jersey City, New Jersey **Teaching Assistant/Lecturer** Prepared curriculum and materials for Freshmen Precalculus and Calculus courses. Served as recitation instructor for Mathematical Analysis up to senior level. Recitation instructor for Logic and Discrete Mathematics. Explained solutions, administered tests and quizzes, and fielded questions about material. • Recipient of "Outstanding Teaching Assistant Award" from student body for both 98-99 and 99-00 school years. • Utilized Maple Computer Software to implement "Studio Calculus." • Presented statistics paper on "Time Series Analysis" to faculty and guests.
1997-1998	SHARPE CAPITAL, New York, New York **Researcher** Responsible for encapsulating financial news in fact sheets for client use.
1995-1997	WILLIAM PATTERSON UNIVERSITY, Wayne, New Jersey **Mathematics Tutor** Tutored in university's "drop-in" math-help center.
CERTIFICATIONS	New Jersey Teaching Certificate in secondary education.
AFFILIATIONS	American Mathematical Society (AMA) Mathematics Association of America (MAA) American Statistical Association (ASA)
COMPUTER SKILLS	Proficient in Microsoft Word, Excel, and PowerPoint; Maple Software (mathematical software package); C++; and FORTRAN.

Figure 3.11: This is an efficient one-page format for an experienced teacher. Note the effective Profile and Summary of Qualifications. (Resume writer: Igor Shpudejko, Mahwah, NJ)

SHARON WELLS

4344 East Franklin Street, Apt. 5
New Haven, Connecticut 06525
(203) 336-8041   Email: germanteach@home.com

GOAL:

High School German Teacher, In-service Instructor, or Computer Technician.

EDUCATION:

Southern Connecticut State University
B.A. Education—Anticipated 2005
Major: **German**
Minor: **Educational Computing & Technology Certificate**—May 2002
GPA: 3.31

Coursework for the Educational Computing & Technology Certificate: The Computer in Education, Teaching with Technology, Utilizing Technology for the Administrative Tasks of Teaching, Current Issues in Computers and Educational Technology, and Advanced Educational Media Production.

COMPUTER SKILLS:

Hardware
Public access terminals, Macintosh and Windows PCs with Ethernet LAN connections, Sun workstations running UNIX operating system, X-terminals, laser and color printers, scanners, video phones, video conferencing, and digital cameras.

Software
MS Word, MS Excel, MS PowerPoint, WordPerfect, ClarisWorks, Claris Home Page, Hyper Studio, Avid Videoshop, Fetch, PageMill, Top Class, PageMaker, QuarkXPress, Photoshop, Swivel 3D, Director, Illustrator, MiniCad, FileMaker Pro, Telnet, Netscape, and TurboGopher.

LANGUAGES:

German. Intermediate to advanced proficiency. Able to read, write, speak, and understand.

VOLUNTEER:

Taught English as a Second Language at the New Haven Adult Learning Center, Fall 2001. Worked in small groups with adults with various languages and 2 Bosnian students.

EXPERIENCE:

2000–Present: **DELI CLERK**
Gala Jubilee, Hamden, CT

Merchandise products, order food, and work events. Relate well to a wide variety of people.

1998–2000: **WAITRESS/CASHIER**
Bonanza, West Haven, CT
Sold more side orders than anyone previously at restaurant. West Haven Bonanza rated top in nation. Performed other tasks as needed.

1997–2002: **VISUAL SPECIALIST MERCHANDISER**
JCPenney, West Hartford, CT
Promoted from Hamden store because of excellent merchandising skills.

Ordered merchandise via computer. Maintained a monthly budget that varied seasonally.

Worked cooperatively with other merchandisers in store as well as district managers.

Continually planned for future events/seasons.

Utilized self-management skills. Managed 2 employees.

1997–1999: **SALES ASSOCIATE**
JCPenney, Hamden, CT
Sold in various departments. Merchandised store products.

Figure 3.12: An unusual format makes this well-organized resume stand out. For a soon-to-be-qualified teacher, education and volunteer activities are as important as work experience. (Resume writer: Linda Wunner)

Jason Lipman

192-37 35th Avenue
Flushing, NY 11351
718-555-9003

Physical Education Teacher (K–12)

- Eager to bring students into the twenty-first century using a unique combination of high-caliber physical education experience and athletic achievement. Will utilize teaching knowledge and more than fifteen years' background as a successful business owner to parallel the development of athletic abilities with the understanding of real-life skills.

- Dedicated to enthusiastic and dynamic teaching as a means of creating a lifelong love of sports and learning in children and young adults. Create an energizing educational experience that motivates students to enjoy physical, academic, and personal accomplishment.

- Trained for a teaching career, but in response to family need, reluctantly put plans aside and joined family business after college (worked in business from age of five). To stay in teaching, took substitute teaching assignments while running business. After fifteen years of profitable business management, have sold business to teach full-time.

Education and Certification

Post-Graduate Coursework
Currently attending Master's in Elementary Education program
St. Joseph's College, Brooklyn, NY

Three-credit Education Course
State University of New York at Stony Brook

Bachelor of Science in Health and Physical Education
Tennessee State University, Yarrow, TN 1983
(attended on full football scholarship)

Undergraduate Coursework
Jefferson Rangle College, Lincoln City, MD
(attended on full football scholarship)

Certification (Provisional, pending renewal)
NY State Physical Education K–12

Key Qualifications

- Experienced college-level coach; worked for five years as defensive line and strength training coach at Hofstra University. Experienced substitute teacher with ability to motivate students in difficult situations.

- As coach and teacher, incorporate learning modality principles into group and individual instruction. Plan, prepare, and instruct in each skills area using wide variety of motivational and implementation strategies to engage students in active learning and accomplishment.

- Possess unique ability to break down components of athletic training into easily assimilated units. Students struggling with techniques become successful after this instructional coaching.

Athletic Achievements

Played two years of semi-pro football for the Elkin Eagles

Tried out for the Giants and the Buffalo Bills

Defensive Line Coach for Hofstra University Bengals Football Team

Hofstra University Strength Training Coach

College Football:

Azalea Bowl MVP
NAIA National Playoffs
Senior Year Team Captain
First Team, All-American
First Team, All-District

High School Football:

All-American
All-State
All-County
All-Long Island
All-League

Figure 3.13: This excellent resume incorporates numerous design elements with a high degree of originality. Because it is well written and well organized, it is easy to skim despite being fairly text-heavy. (Resume writer: Deborah Wile Dib, Medford, NY)

Jason Lipman   2

Employment in Education

Substitute Teacher (grades 1–12), New York, NY   **1989 to present**

- **New York City Schools**
- **Sewhanaka School District**
- **St. Kevin's Elementary School, Elmont, NY**

Teach academic subjects and all physical education activities including indoor baseball, wiffle ball, basketball, and volleyball. Handle difficult assignments by developing a mutual respect with students and deflecting natural aggression towards substitutes. Utilize personal style of instruction that enhances motivation and reduces opportunities for student disruption. Create an energized atmosphere that generates interest and participation.

Defensive Line Coach for Hofstra Bengals Football Team
Weight Lifting Coach
Hofstra University, Hempstead, NY   **1983 to 1988**

As Defensive Line Coach, taught techniques and form; made up daily practice schedules and routines; set up film appointments for players and graded players by films. Reviewed game plans, incorporating defense and offense. Handled scouting and recruiting for New York and New Jersey teams; wrote scouting reports and attended team meetings. Taught visualization techniques for instinctive, reactive play.

As Weight Lifting Coach, attended NSCA convention; learned and incorporated cutting-edge conditioning strategies into workouts that encouraged college athletes to do total-body conditioning between sets. Developed jump-rope program that dramatically increased athletes' agility.

Student Teaching

Health and Physical Education (grades 7–12)
Johnstown Middle School and High School, Raleigh, ND   **1983**

Offered permanent position; declined due to family responsibilities. As student teacher, instructed students in football, weight training, and track. Used motivation and skills coaching to develop shot put ability in student struggling with technique; student qualified for state championship.

Health and Physical Education (grades K–12)
Hopewell School, Hopewell, TN   **1983**

Business Ownership

Owner/Partner/Operator
All-State Carting, Maspeth, NY   **1983 to 2001**

Recently sold business to a major public company in waste management. All-State was a six-partner waste management company with its own transfer station facility and was aggressively involved in the management/disposal of recycling, municipal solid waste, and construction/demolition debris.

Note: Keep a record of every resume you send or hand-deliver. Be especially careful to save a copy of any resume that you have customized for a specific job vacancy.

If, after looking at these samples, you still feel unsure about writing your resume, contact your college career placement office. There you'll find professionals trained to help you.

Impressive Cover Letters

You should never send an application or a resume without a cover letter. Not all applicants know the importance of cover letters (also known as "letters of intent"), but if you take the time to include one with your application, the extra touch of professionalism will increase your chances of making the paper cut. All else being equal, the principal will select applicants who have the most professional presentations. An impressive cover letter will help you be one of those applicants.

Here are some general guidelines to use when composing a cover letter:

- The letter should be the original (no photocopies) and should be printed on a quality printer. *Never send a handwritten letter.*
- Use high-quality white or off-white 8½ × 11 paper.
- Use perfect grammar.
- No typos or misspelled words are allowed.
- Never address the letter "Dear Sir," "Dear Madam," or "To Whom It May Concern." Make a telephone call to find out exactly who should receive your letter, along with the person's title and the correct spelling of his or her name.

Figure 3.14 is a template for the suggested content of the letter.

Your Name
Your Address

Today's Date

Name of the Administrator or Personnel Director
Name of School District
Street Address or P. O. Box
City, State, ZIP Code

Dear _____:

State the purpose of the letter (to be considered for any positions that may become available, or for a specific position that has been advertised).

Tell them what your status is now and why you feel you would be especially well qualified for this position. (This is a chance to tell them about one of your strengths.)

This paragraph should include one or two brief sentences that emphasize your passion for teaching and your love for kids.

If possible, it is always nice to personalize your letter by saying something positive about the community or school district and why you would like to work there. (When you call to ask for the name of the person to whom the letter should be sent, ask if the district or city has a Web address. If so, this will tell you what the city and district have to offer.)

Let them know that you have arranged to have a copy of your transcript and letters of reference forwarded to them. Thank them for their time and consideration.

Sincerely,

Your Name

Figure 3.14: A cover letter template.

Your cover letter, like any business letter, should be tailored to each specific job vacancy. The sample cover letter in figure 3.15 was written by Karen McCrae. She has tailored her letter to a specific job vacancy: "High school history and social studies teacher; assistant coach—girls' varsity basketball."

Karen McCrae
2117 Bennington Way
Taylorville, IL 60005

May 3, 2007

Dr. Richard Fagan, Principal
Laketown High School
Laketown, IL 60048

Dear Dr. Fagan:

Please consider me as an applicant for the 11th-grade history/social studies position that will be available this coming fall. I learned of this vacancy from my college placement office at Lincoln University, where I will earn my bachelor's degree on June 5 with a major in history and a minor in French.

I notice that your job announcement includes adjunct duties as girls' assistant basketball coach. This is of great interest to me, not only because of my past experience playing and coaching women's basketball, but because it would give me one more opportunity to fulfill my passion to make a difference in students' lives by showing them respect and building their self-esteem. When my students are my age, I want to be the one who stands out in their memories because I really cared.

Although I have visited Laketown several times, I never knew until recently of your high school's fine academic reputation. I notice that 89 percent of your graduates go on to college. The community must be very proud of its high school, and rightfully so.

I look forward to hearing from you soon and meeting with you personally at your convenience. I can be reached at (708) 555-1908.

Sincerely,

Karen McCrae

Figure 3.15: A sample cover letter.

If you were Dr. Fagan and had a stack of applications sitting on your desk, wouldn't this well-written cover letter catch your attention? It would be especially impressive if none of the other applicants had bothered to include one.

Winning Applications

After all the work you've done up to this point—assessing your strengths and weaknesses, preparing your mission statement, and writing your resume—the application itself might seem like a piece of cake. Unfortunately, it is not.

> "Take your application seriously—it's an initial representation of yourself."
> —Secondary English teacher who has served on interview committees in Ohio

Your application, like your resume, is a representation of you—serious stuff! If a district's personnel office receives more than 100 applications for a teaching vacancy (which is common in many school districts), the staff has only so much time to scan each one in the stack. These people are sharp, however: Their eyes are trained, and they can rule out many applicants after only a quick glance at the applications. They do this based not only on the content of the applications but on how neatly and carefully they were prepared. Therefore, you want your application to make the best impression possible so that it will work for you rather than against you.

The following sections show you how to make yours a winning application.

Gather the Information You Will Need

The first step is to gather all the information you will need to fill out the application:

- **Educational background,** with dates attended and graduated, GPA, honors, and so on
- **Professional experience,** with dates and addresses
- **Other work experience,** with dates, addresses, and reasons for leaving
- **Teaching credentials** held and their expiration dates
- **Professional references,** including addresses and telephone numbers
- **Personal information,** including Social Security number, passport number, driver's license number, and so on
- **Honors, awards, and fellowships** you have received
- **Special skills** or related experiences

As you gather this information, enter it on an actual application form; that way, you'll have everything together in one place when you need it. Figure 3.16 is a sample application you can use for this purpose.

LAKETOWN HIGH SCHOOL
Laketown, Illinois

Regular _____
Substitute _____
Home Teaching _____

CERTIFICATED APPLICATION
Personnel Services: (501) 555-8000
FAX: (501) 555-8004
AN EQUAL OPPORTUNITY EMPLOYER

FOR PERSONNEL OFFICE USE
Entry Date _____
By _____

PERSONAL:

Last Name _____ First Name _____ M.I. _____ Social Security No. _____

Present
Address _____ Phone ( ) _____
(Street)

(City and State) _____ (Zip) _____

Permanent
Address _____ Phone ( ) _____
(Street)

(City and State) _____ (Zip) _____

POSITION DESIRED:

Level Preference: List subject and/or grade level of preference:

_____ ELEMENTARY (K-5) _____

_____ MIDDLE (6-8) _____

_____ HIGH SCHOOL (9-12) _____

_____ OTHER _____

Please list other languages you speak: _____

FOR PERSONNEL OFFICE USE

ILLINOIS CREDENTIAL INFORMATION: Expiration Date

Illinois Credentials now held _____ _____

_____ _____

If no Illinois credential now, have you applied for one? YES _____ NO _____

What type? _____ When? _____

Do you hold an out-of-state credential?

YES ___ NO ___ What type? _____ State _____

EDUCATION AND PROFESSIONAL TRAINING: (College or University only)

Name and Location of Institution Attended	Dates Attended From	To	Major(s)	Minor	Graduation Date – Degrees

TEACHING AND/OR ADMINISTRATIVE EXPERIENCE:

Total years of full-time, paid teaching experience: _____ Total years of administrative and/or supervisory experience:_____ LIST ALL EXPERIENCE BY POSITIONS IN CHRONOLOGICAL ORDER. ADMINISTRATORS NEED NOT LIST STUDENT TEACHING. FOR TEACHER APPLICANTS, LIST STUDENT TEACHING FIRST. DO NOT COUNT STUDENT TEACHING IN TOTAL YEARS TAUGHT.

Dates	Location (City/State)	Name/Level of School	Grade or Subjects Taught	Salary
				Student Teaching

Figure 3.16: A sample application.

Be positive and creative as you enter the information on the application form. For example, when entering previous job titles, responsibilities, and reasons for leaving, use the most glowing terms possible without compromising the truth. You should also use as many power verbs as possible (see the list earlier in this chapter).

For example, suppose you worked one summer emptying trash and vacuuming the halls of an office building after closing time each business day. You might say "Maintained and secured building." (Surely you locked up when you left, didn't you?) The words "maintained" and "secured" are power verbs.

If you have a gimmicky, cute message on your answering machine, replace it with something more professional, like this: "You have reached 555–9085. Please leave a message at the beep." The reason is obvious: When schools start calling to set up interviews, you don't want to make a bad impression before they even meet you.

Another good idea is to target your application in much the same way as you would a resume, by including any skills, training, awards, work experiences, or activities that match the job vacancy you want to fill. This is a way to "load" the application in your favor so that you appear more qualified than the other applicants.

As you indulge in this "creative writing," always choose your words carefully, and never use more words than necessary—they clutter up the page.

Completing the Application

It's always best to type an application, if you can get your hands on a typewriter these days. Otherwise, print as neatly as you can, using a black or dark-blue ballpoint pen. If you're visiting various schools and personnel offices as part of your school survey, and you are handed an application to fill out, if possible, take it home with you instead of filling it out on the spot. That way, you can take your time to complete it and proofread it carefully before actually submitting it. As a precaution, we suggest making a copy of the application, filling out the copy first as a rough draft, and then recopying your information onto the original form.

"Pay attention to details. Never send in an application with even one single typo!" —Instructional coordinator and member of the interview committee for a suburban district in Virginia

However, if time is of the essence and it's imperative that you complete the application then and there, be sure to print, using an erasable black pen. (If you're lucky, a typewriter might be furnished for you to use.) Always carry an erasable pen, your sample application, and a small dictionary in your briefcase so that you'll be prepared with the information and tools you need in case you can't take the application home with you.

> **Tip:** Many school districts have their applications available online at their Web sites. If this is true for the school district to which you are applying, go to its Web site and complete the application online. Then you can either print it to submit with your resume in person, or you can submit it online. Some districts also offer the option of pasting your own resume into their form online.

Whether you type or print your application, be sure it's error-free and has no misspelled words.

An application that has every section completed in a clear, easy-to-read way, with no typos or misspelled words, has an excellent chance of making the paper cut.

We've included two applications that were filled out by Karen McCrae. Her first application was very poorly prepared. Not only was it handwritten, it was messy and incomplete. There were several errors, including her home address and the information about her teaching credential. Her second try was much better: neatly typed, complete, and error-free.

If you were the personnel director of a large school district, which one would you put at the top of the pile?

LAKETOWN HIGH SCHOOL
Laketown, Illinois
CERTIFICATED APPLICATION
Personnel Services: (501) 555-8000
FAX: (501) 555-8004
AN EQUAL OPPORTUNITY EMPLOYER

Regular _____
Substitute _____
Home Teaching _____

FOR PERSONNEL OFFICE USE
Entry Date _____
By _____

PERSONAL:

McCrae, Karen A.   Social Security No. *556-07-1131*
Last Name   First Name   M.I.

Present Address *2117 Bennington Way*   Phone *708 555-1908*
(Street)

Taylorville, ILL 60005
(City and State)   (Zip)

Permanent Address *206 Lavenne Way*   Phone *708 276-4415*
(Street)

Taylorville, IL 60215
(City and State)   (Zip)

FOR PERSONNEL OFFICE USE

POSITION DESIRED:

Level Preference: List subject and/or grade level of preference:

____ ELEMENTARY (K-5)

✗ MIDDLE (6-8)

✗ HIGH SCHOOL (9-12)   *History French*

✓ OTHER   *Girls Basketball/Volleyball Coach*

Please list other languages you speak: *Spanish French*

ILLINOIS CREDENTIAL INFORMATION: Expiration Date

Illinois Credentials now held *Secondary Teaching* *6/2007*

If no Illinois credential now, have you applied for one? YES ____ NO ✓

What type? _____ When? _____

Do you hold an out-of-state credential?

YES ___ NO ___ What type? _____ State _____

EDUCATION AND PROFESSIONAL TRAINING: (College or University only)

Name and Location of Institution Attended	Dates Attended From	To	Major(s)	Minor	Graduation Date – Degrees
Lincoln University Arlington Heights, IL	*9/99*	*6/03*	*History*	*French*	*2003 BA History*
Weth					

TEACHING AND/OR ADMINISTRATIVE EXPERIENCE:

Total years of full-time, paid teaching experience: _____ Total years of administrative and/or supervisory experience: _____ LIST ALL EXPERIENCE BY POSITIONS IN CHRONOLOGICAL ORDER. ADMINISTRATORS NEED NOT LIST STUDENT TEACHING. FOR TEACHER APPLICANTS, LIST STUDENT TEACHING FIRST. DO NOT COUNT STUDENT TEACHING IN TOTAL YEARS TAUGHT.

Dates	Location (City/State)	Name/Level of School	Grade or Subjects Taught	Salary
1/03-6/03	*Oakmont, IL*	*Oakmont High 9-12*	*10 U.S. History 11 World History*	Student Teaching

Figure 3.17: Karen's messy application form.

LAKETOWN HIGH SCHOOL
Laketown, Illinois

Regular ___X___
Substitute _____
Home Teaching _____

CERTIFICATED APPLICATION
Personnel Services: (501) 555-8000
FAX: (501) 555-8004

AN EQUAL OPPORTUNITY EMPLOYER

FOR PERSONNEL OFFICE USE
Entry Date _____
By _____

PERSONAL:

McCrae   Karen   A.   Social Security No. _556-07-1131_
Last Name   First Name   M.I.

Present
Address ___2117 Bennington Way___   Phone (708) _555-1908_
                        (Street)

_____Taylorville, Ill._____ ___60005___
        (City and State)   (Zip)

Permanent _206 Lavern Way_   Phone (708) _276-4415_
Address
                        (Street)

_____Taylorville, Ill._____ ___60215___
        (City and State)   (Zip)

FOR PERSONNEL OFFICE USE

POSITION DESIRED:

Level Preference: List subject and/or grade level of preference:

____ ELEMENTARY (K-5)

____ MIDDLE (6-8)

_X_ HIGH SCHOOL (9-12)   History, French

_X_ OTHER   Girl's basketball/Volleyball coach

Please list other languages you speak: Spanish / French

ILLINOIS CREDENTIAL INFORMATION: Expiration Date

Illinois Credentials now held _____   _____

_____   _____

If no Illinois credential now, have you applied for one? **YES** ____ **NO** ____

What type? _General Secondary_ When? _June 2007_

Do you hold an out-of-state credential?

        YES ___ **NO** _X_ What type? _____ State _____

EDUCATION AND PROFESSIONAL TRAINING: (College or University only)

Name and Location of Institution Attended	Dates Attended From	To	Major(s)	Minor	Graduation Date – Degrees
Lincoln University Arlington Heights, IL	9/99	6/03	History	French	June, 2003 B.A.
Taylorville Community College Taylorville, Illinois	9/96	6/99	History	None	June, 2000 A.A.

TEACHING AND/OR ADMINISTRATIVE EXPERIENCE:

Total years of full-time, paid teaching experience: _____ Total years of administrative and/or supervisory experience:_____ LIST ALL EXPERIENCE BY POSITIONS IN CHRONOLOGICAL ORDER. ADMINISTRATORS NEED NOT LIST STUDENT TEACHING. FOR TEACHER APPLICANTS, LIST STUDENT TEACHING FIRST. DO NOT COUNT STUDENT TEACHING IN TOTAL YEARS TAUGHT.

Dates	Location (City/State)	Name/Level of School	Grade or Subjects Taught	Salary
1/03-6/03	Craymont, IL	Craymont High School 9-12	10-U.S. History 11-World History	Student Teaching
(Also coached girls' basketball; computer research)				Stud. Teach.
9/02-12/02	Newport, IL	Treyton High School	History; French; girls' volleyball	Stud. Teach.

Figure 3.18: A much neater and more acceptable version of Karen's application.

Sterling References

You'll need four to six letters of reference for your job search. Typically, these are written by people who can attest to your character and teaching ability. They're usually sent to your college or university career placement office to be included in your professional file. That way, they're all together in one place, ready to be sent out when a potential employer requests them.

You have a right to see any and all references placed in your professional file. If any are of questionable value, you may have them removed. Your placement office staff will help you evaluate all the letters that come in. If it's determined that a letter is to be removed, you must follow your placement center's procedures. An undesirable letter might be removed from your file and destroyed, or it might be placed in an inactive file, where it will not be sent with your other letters of recommendation.

The two kinds of reference letters are professional and personal. The following sections discuss each type.

Professional Reference Letters

Early in your career, professional letters of recommendation usually are written by people who have direct knowledge of your student-teaching ability. These include college professors, college supervisors, and master teachers. As you gain experience, these letters will be replaced with new letters written by department heads, principals, superintendents, and fellow teachers.

Personal Reference Letters

Personal letters of recommendation are an important part of your file, especially when you're just getting started in your career. They generally are written by people who know you well and can share insights into your character and values. These could include former teachers, counselors, coaches, administrators, members of the clergy, neighbors, and leaders of youth organizations.

Professional letters of recommendation are written by people who are familiar with the process; they typically have written many of these letters, and they know exactly what is expected in the way of content and format. This might not be the case with personal letters. When you ask someone for a personal letter of recommendation, pay careful attention to the person's response. If he or she isn't quite sure how to go about it, offer to furnish copies of the letters you've already received. These will be a big help in terms of wording and format.

When your professional file is full of reference letters, it's up to you to maintain the file by periodically requesting new or updated letters of recommendation. This way your file is always fresh and up to date.

By the way, one of the biggest mistakes new teacher candidates make is to wait until the last minute to request these reference letters. Be aware that people don't always write them on a moment's notice, even if they have the best intentions of doing so. Some procrastinate because they're on overload at the moment and don't have time to write a letter; others are forgetful or might lose your original request.

Also, it's important to remember that a professor or supervisor might have 20 other letters to write, so be considerate. And then there's Murphy's Law, which says that when you need to reach someone the most, that person is on hiatus, is traveling down the Amazon, or is recovering from surgery and is not due back in the office for six weeks. So make your requests as early as possible; you'll be glad you did.

When your references are in, make a few extra copies to slip into your portfolio so that you'll have them with you during your interviews. You typically won't hand these out at interviews, or even be asked for them, but who knows? It can't hurt to have them handy.

If you pass the paper cut with your application and resume, *these letters will be requested.* Their content might determine whether you make it to the interview table.

CHAPTER 4

The Inside Track: Student Teaching, Volunteering, Subbing, and Temping

There are several ways to find the "inside track." You can impress key people on a school's campus as you student-teach, work as a volunteer, serve as a substitute, or fill a temporary teaching vacancy. If you do an outstanding job in any of these positions, you're sure to be noticed by the principal, your master teacher, and others who have hiring authority or can recommend you to those who do. Don't pass up a chance to showcase yourself!

Be an Enthusiastic Student Teacher

Your student-teaching experience is an important part of your job search. The evaluations from your university supervisor, master teacher, school site principal, and others are the most important references you'll have in your placement file, because they're from professional educators who've seen your performance in the classroom or have been closely associated with it. These are the people who've evaluated your lessons, classroom-management skills, and everything you've been trained to do over the last few years. These people, for now, hold your professional life in their hands. You'd better do your best to impress them!

If you're already a credentialed teacher who's completed your student teaching, you don't need to be reminded of the importance of a good, solid student-teaching performance that results in great evaluations and letters of reference. But if you have your student teaching ahead of you, or if you're in the middle of it, you should try to impress *anyone* in a position to write letters of reference for your placement file.

Of the newly hired teachers in our survey, 6 percent were hired at the schools where they did their student teaching.

You might not be particularly interested in staying in the district where you're student-teaching, but the impressions you make there will follow you wherever you go. And if you *are* interested in the district where you're doing your student teaching, keep in mind that if they like you they won't want to lose you to another district! As we researched this book, that fact was made abundantly clear—and it makes sense. After all, the administrators in that district *know* you; they've seen what you can bring to their schools and to their kids. So if you make a positive impression on the teachers and administrators, they'll want you somewhere in their district. It's a win-win situation!

Give Them Something Extra

In most student-teaching situations, you're given a prescribed schedule to follow. For instance, in your first week or so you'll probably observe your master teacher and get to know the students in your class. You'll gradually take on more teaching responsibilities until you "go solo," when you take over the class and your master teacher stays behind the scenes as much as possible. Then, toward the end of your assignment, the master teacher will ease back into the teaching scene to smooth the transition when your solo stint is over.

Here's some helpful advice as you begin your student-teaching experience: From the very start, even during the observation period, make creative suggestions for things you can do to help your master teacher. For example, you might suggest such things as constructing a bulletin board, handling the attendance duties, or taking the lunch count. Also, think of any skills you have that are related to teaching. (Remember the transferable skills we talked about in chapter 1?) These will help you develop a relationship with the kids, as well as showcase something special you can bring to the classroom.

If you're artistically talented, for example, you can add something to the room environment. If you play the guitar, think of a fun song you can teach the class. If the students are older and don't think it's cool to sing "Puff the Magic Dragon," think of another, more age-appropriate song. The point is this: If you follow your prescribed student-teaching schedule to the letter and you never offer anything special, you're missing an opportunity to showcase yourself and begin the process of "selling your product," even at this early stage.

Another Chance to Network

Another good idea is to create a network with other student teachers at your school, sharing information and getting to know them well. This can really pay off when you're further along in your job search. (We'll talk more about this valuable idea in chapter 6.)

Don't limit your networking to your fellow student teachers, however. The principal, assistant principal, and mentor teachers can all help you land that plum teaching job. And never underestimate the power and influence of school secretaries—you can take it to the bank that they know what's going on! Definitely befriend them.

Your network should include the full-time teachers at the school as well. They often know influential people within the district. You never know—one of them might even be a close friend, a spouse, or related to someone in the district with hiring authority. We heard from several student teachers and substitute teachers in our survey who took advantage of these contacts to land great teaching positions.

So take your student-teaching experience seriously. Plan on putting in long days and going the extra mile. Get to the classroom early, and be there every school day. Take advantage of every opportunity to teach and interact with students. Be dedicated; be enthusiastic.

Get Good Letters of Reference

The most important letter of reference you'll have in your placement file is the one from your master teacher. After all, that person has worked more closely with you on a daily basis than anyone else. Make it easy for him or her to write an excellent letter.

> "You should have outstanding recommendations, so work hard at whatever you do, and go above and beyond while you're a student teacher."
> —Member of an interview committee in Miami, Florida

Here are two examples of what your master teacher might say:

> *"Cliff Johnson was a student teacher in my classroom during the spring semester of 2003. His attendance was satisfactory, and he was usually punctual. He maintained adequate classroom control. His lessons indicated planning...."*

or

> *"Cliff Johnson was a student teacher in my classroom during the spring semester of 2003. He arrived early and stayed late every school day. His classroom control was excellent. He enthusiastically presented well-prepared lessons...."*

If you were screening applications and ran across these two letters, which would impress you more? The answer is obvious. We can't overemphasize the importance of your student-teaching experience and its impact on your job search.

If you do a good job, people will hear about you. Principals talk to other principals, teachers talk to teachers, parents talk to parents. It's like a pebble thrown into a pond, making concentric waves. Never underestimate the role of chance in getting a job. Think of all the people you know who got their jobs in some strange way: "So-and-so" knew "so-and-so," who heard from "so-and-so" about a job over in Pikeville. You might say the more so-and-sos who know you, the better chance you have of getting a job!

Become an Enthusiastic School Volunteer

Doing volunteer work at a school is another way to make yourself known. If you have something to offer young people in the classroom, this will show up when you volunteer to help out at a school. The more exposure you get within the educational community, the better your chances of becoming known by those with hiring authority.

For starters, think about joining the school's parent-teacher organization. Not only will you get to know the school's principal and teachers, but they'll recognize your commitment to kids and education. They'll also get a sense of your attitude and work ethic.

If you become a classroom volunteer as well, you'll have many ways to impress a particular teacher as you showcase your skills, talents, and love of children. For example, if you accompany the class on a field trip and help the teacher cope with the inevitable mini-crises that happen along the way, you'll create a positive impression, and you can count on your excellent reputation filtering back to the principal and other teachers at the school.

At the secondary level, take whatever special talents you have—whether in drama, music, athletics, foreign languages, or fund-raising—and volunteer to use them in some way. You might volunteer as a chaperone for school dances. Or you might work with a class on their yearbook, coordinate homecoming activities, or help plan the decorations for the junior-senior prom. There are dozens of ways to help out—it just takes some creative thinking, initiative, and effort on your part.

By offering your services as a school volunteer, not only will you help the kids and staff, you'll put yourself on the inside track to teaching vacancies as they come up—and that's the bottom line. Look at it this way: School volunteerism is just one more way to keep your "net working." After all, the more territory your net covers, the more you make yourself known—and, as you've already learned, the first rule of the job search is *to become known!*

Become an Enthusiastic Sub or Temp

As we researched this book, we talked to many teachers who were hired by the school or district where they had worked as substitute teachers. Some had subbed on a day-to-day basis; others had filled part-time or temporary positions. If you're having trouble finding a full-time job, this might be the route for you.

Short-Term Subbing

If you decide to try subbing, it's important to be available when a school calls. If you give the school your cell phone number, and you make sure you always have your phone with you, you can go about your day as usual.

> Of the newly hired teachers in our survey, 13 percent were hired for full-time positions at the schools where they had worked as substitute teachers.

To get your name on the sub list, call the school district's personnel office, which will inform you of the district's policies. Every district's policies are a little different. If you have your heart set on subbing at only one or two specific schools, you might need to state that when you call the personnel office, or you might need to call the school itself, because some schools have their own sub lists.

Usually you'll be called before 7 a.m. Someone from the school or sub service will ask if you're available to take a certain class for that day. You always have the option to decline, of course, and on occasion you'll have to, for any number of reasons. But if you want to maintain a good working relationship with a district, don't make a habit of turning them down. If you do, they'll stop calling. Of course, if you're signed up to sub with several districts, there will be times you're forced to decline one job because you've already taken another, which is one of the disadvantages of spreading yourself too thin.

When you do get called to fill in as a sub, do a good job. Here are some hints for being a good sub:

- Be on time.
- Be prepared.
- Treat the class as if it were your own.
- Maintain control—don't let the students walk all over you.
- Try to accomplish all the regular teacher's lesson plans for the day.
- Leave detailed notes and comments on your progress. Keep these comments as upbeat and positive as possible, but don't be afraid to let the teacher know about any students who misbehaved.

Tip: Recall times when as a student you had substitute teachers. What did they do to achieve success or cause failure?

You need to realize that the teacher/substitute relationship is a symbiotic one. The teacher depends on you to carry out that day's lesson plans. But you, as a substitute teacher in the midst of a job hunt, are actually more dependent on the teacher than the teacher is on you. After all, the teacher already has a full-time job, and you don't. The point is this: It's important for you to impress the teacher by doing a superior job of subbing.

If you develop a reputation for doing your best to carry out the teacher's lesson plans, taking time to jot down notes, and maintaining good control over the classroom, your reputation will spread fast around the district. Having such a reputation certainly gives you a leg up on your competition when it comes to landing a full-time job.

Note: Several excellent books on substitute teaching are available at your local teacher-supply store. These are usually inexpensive and are very helpful for the beginning substitute teacher.

When you serve as a short- or long-term substitute teacher, you become *known* in the school and the district, and becoming *known* is the number one goal of all job seekers, regardless of the profession. Many teacher candidates sign up to sub in several different districts, in fact, multiplying their chances to become known for their teaching skills, their ability to get along with parents and staff, and their enthusiasm and flexibility. Often, these substitutes get called to one school or another every day of the week.

Long-Term Subbing

If you agree to take on a temporary position (also known as long-term subbing), you have an even better chance to shine by impressing your fellow teachers, the secretaries, mentor teachers, and administrators over a longer period of time. Many teachers seek out temporary positions for this very reason, especially if the school or district is one where they would be happy in a full-time position.

What many teacher candidates don't realize is that those who accept temporary positions are often placed in a hiring pool for full-time positions that become available in the future. In fact, one administrator in the San Francisco Bay area told us that *all* new teaching positions are offered first to those in the temporary and part-time hiring pool from the previous year. We also heard of several cases in which teachers had to leave the classroom for personal or health reasons and were unable to return. The substitutes who took over and did a good job in those situations had the inside track when the job vacancies were officially advertised.

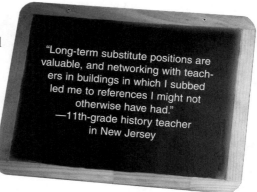

"Long-term substitute positions are valuable, and networking with teachers in buildings in which I subbed led me to references I might not otherwise have had."
—11th-grade history teacher in New Jersey

As long-time teachers and administrators, we can vouch for the fact that short- and long-term subbing often leads to a full-time position. It is a great method to get yourself *known* and eventually hired.

Think of your subbing experience as another way to extend your network every time you're called to a new school. Any teacher, principal, or secretary you impress with your attitude and professionalism could be your pipeline to that ideal teaching position.

Be patient and persistent. And if you choose substitute teaching as a bridge to your own full-time position, just remember that subbing will make you that much better prepared for the exciting day when you walk into your very own classroom. And you will—it's coming soon!

CHAPTER 5

The Nontraditional Path: Help for Non-Education Majors and Those Returning to the Field

We're all familiar with the adage "It's a matter of being in the right place at the right time." Well, this is particularly relevant to the current situation in the teaching field, where school districts are desperate to fill their teaching vacancies and there aren't enough qualified candidates. That's where career switchers and teachers who are returning to the profession after a long absence come in.

Why Do You Want to Be a Teacher?

Why do so many people change careers at this stage of their lives? These are the reasons they have given us:

- They're retiring from their current profession, many with full retirement benefits, and they want a meaningful second career.
- They were laid off after a round of corporate downsizing, and they have decided to pursue teaching, which is perceived as a more stable area.
- They are unfulfilled in their current career.
- They are working mothers who have been in high-stress careers that demand long hours and lots of overtime. They have decided to pursue a teaching career, where the hours are similar to their kids' schedules. (A word of caution: While you may share vacation schedules, teachers' work-days typically are long.)

If you're returning to the teaching profession after being out of it for many years, you might be coming back for one of the following reasons:

- You tried out a different profession, but you didn't find it rewarding.
- You've been unemployed for a number of years, perhaps serving as a stay-at-home parent, and now you must seek employment because your spouse was laid off. Or your kids might be grown and out of the house, and this is your time to enjoy a career of your own.

Also, research has shown that many who are now seeking to enter the teaching profession are doing so because of 9/11. That tragedy caused many people to rethink their priorities and to want to spend the rest of their lives contributing in a meaningful way. And is there a more meaningful and rewarding profession than teaching?

It's interesting that a recent open house for mid-career switchers held by the Bank Street College of Education in New York saw a record turnout of people who are rethinking their lives and wanting to get into the teaching field.

> IBM Corporation is committed to helping the nation's schools recruit qualified people to teach math and science. It provides employees with salaries and benefits while they take the necessary courses to become teachers. It also pays tuition costs up to $15,000.

If you fall into any of these categories, we have wonderful news for you: You're definitely in the right place at the right time. This is your golden opportunity to secure a teaching position.

School Districts Are Seeking Second-Career and Returning Teachers

School districts are looking for people in their 40s and 50s who have retired from their first career or who have given up on their first career because it wasn't satisfying. Many of these candidates are retired military or government workers who have all their retirement benefits and are looking for a rewarding, fulfilling second career. The districts are also seeking out teachers who are returning to the profession after a lengthy absence.

Fortunately, nontraditional teacher candidates have less difficulty finding a teaching position because school-district administrators like them. They find that older first-year instructors bring more life experience to the classroom than the traditional 22-year-old college graduate.

One administrator said that he's found that an older person has been in the real world and can tell the students what to expect. Another said that career switchers bring a wealth of experience and a sense of dedication to the task. Mothers who have raised families and obtained a teaching credential along the way usually make excellent teachers. The experience they bring to the classroom is invaluable.

Creative Incentives

School districts have such an astounding shortage of teachers that they're coming up with all kinds of creative incentives to entice applicants:

- Signing bonuses and stipends, especially for bilingual teachers, math teachers, and science teachers
- Low-interest mortgages
- Low-cost housing
- Discounts at local businesses, including dry cleaners and auto-repair shops
- Reimbursement of college expenses
- Van shuttles to transport teachers from their homes to their teaching jobs
- Recruitment of student teachers who have barely started their student-teaching assignments, moving them directly into available positions before they have received their teaching credentials

The city and county of San Francisco recently hired 500 teachers who do not have their full teaching credentials.

- Recruitment of career switchers, placing them into existing positions while they pursue their teaching credentials outside of their school responsibilities
- Recruitment of foreign teachers, including sponsoring work visas, which are good for up to six years
- Recruitment of former military personnel

Universities, colleges, and the federal government are also coming up with innovative ways to get more career switchers and returning teachers trained and ready to fill positions:

- Colleges and universities are implementing fast-track teacher-preparation programs.
- School districts are developing programs to help career switchers and returning teachers make an easy transition into current teaching positions.

- The Defense Department has developed the Troops to Teachers Program and E-March, a campaign to snag soon-to-retire military officers. It also has created teacher-recruitment ventures such as the Army Transition Project, a joint venture between the military and the Florida Department of Education.

> If you are transitioning from the military to a civilian career, check out *Expert Resumes for Military-to-Civilian Transitions* (JIST Works, 2006). This helpful book contains tips on writing a career-transition resume that focuses on your transferable skills and creating a theme-related document that presents a picture of how you want to be perceived by your interviewer.

Programs for Recruiting and Training New Teachers from Other Fields

Most states allow career switchers who don't have a B.A. in education to teach on a temporary basis. However, such individuals are usually required to become certified within one or two years. We know of teachers who take several one- or two-day classes during the summer and evening classes during the school year, plus teach summer-school courses under the guidance of certified teachers. With all this combined training, they expect to become certified teachers within two years.

Many school districts around the country are developing their own fast-track programs for career switchers and returning teachers who are transitioning back into the teaching profession. For example, San Jose's Teaching Fellows Program provides coaching and mentors to work with career switchers who have B.A.s in other fields. Jennifer, a former dot-commer who did not have a teaching credential, was placed in a seventh- and eighth-grade teaching position. With the help of the Teaching Fellows Program, she is working toward her credential.

New York City, which has the largest school district in the nation, recently solicited mid-career professionals through its Teaching Fellows Program. School-district officials were surprised to have more than 2,300 applicants. After only a monthlong training session, 325 of these applicants were chosen to teach in the city's classrooms. Meanwhile, these applicants are also enrolled in an accelerated master's degree program. Surprisingly, these applicants included lawyers, doctors, and a retired judge.

The city of Chicago has launched a Global Educators Outreach Program, which has provided teachers from India, Colombia, and the Philippines. Many of these teachers were college professors in their home countries.

Tucson, Arizona is hiring career switchers who have graduated from the University of Arizona's Teach for Tucson's fast-track program. This program leads to a master's degree in education and a teacher certification in only a year. The University of Arizona received more than 800 inquiries for the first 30 openings when the program debuted in May 2000. To date the program has produced hundreds of secondary-education and elementary teachers. Preference is given to applicants with some type of undergraduate background in math, science, or Spanish, although fast-track programs throughout the United States are graduating teachers in all fields of study, including general elementary.

> Teach for Tucson has tapped an essentially unaddressed niche —"the mid-career professional who perhaps had very successful experiences, but maybe part of that experience was not as fulfilling as they thought it might be."
> —Robert Hendricks, Assistant Dean for Professional Preparation, University of Arizona College of Education

North Carolina is another excellent example of a state that's had to develop an innovative program to train more teachers. This state has worked with its teacher colleges to establish a Grow Your Own Teacher Program. The goal of this program is to provide teacher-education courses for students who are isolated from colleges and universities by providing visiting professors, long-distance education over the Internet, and live videoconference classes.

Nontraditional students are making the transition to fast-track college teaching programs very quickly, taking less time to graduate than students in their 20s and making better grades than typical college students. Also, because nontraditional students are often on very tight budgets, they are highly focused. Their motto is "Get in, study hard, get out, and find a teaching job." These students aren't concerned about joining a fraternity or sorority, and they couldn't care less about Homecoming festivities. They're in this for one purpose: to become qualified to teach and to be employed as quickly as possible.

As far as the Defense Department goes, currently about a million veterans are close to retirement. Many of them are too young to retire permanently and want to do something else with their lives until they reach permanent retirement age. Many will take advantage of the Troops to Teachers Program and become teachers.

> More than 12 percent of all newly hired teachers enter classrooms without any training.
> —National Commission on Teaching and America's Future

A Teacher Needs Many Skills That You Probably Already Have

Not only must a teacher be a multitalented person, but teaching is a multidimensional profession. In our first book, *The Unauthorized Teacher's Survival Guide,* we discuss how a teacher is required to wear many hats during any given day in the classroom:

- Surrogate parent
- Friend
- Social worker
- Provider
- Psychologist
- Nurse
- Emergency worker

As you can see from this list, you undoubtedly have experience in many of these capacities, because you might have raised a family, dealt with coworkers, been a friend to a neighbor in need, or served as an amateur paramedic at the scene of an accident.

Actually, any career experience you've had to date involves skills and talents that are transferable to the classroom. Take a look at the success stories at the end of this chapter, where you'll see examples of career switchers whose talents and skills were easily adapted to the field of teaching.

Marketing Your Related Life Experiences and Transferable Skills

You now know that there is a huge demand for teachers, and you've also seen that school districts seek out career switchers and returning teachers. So, this being true, how can you market yourself when you have little or no teaching experience? The answer is to play your "spin doctor" card by juicing up your cover letter, resume, and personal interview. The key is to sell your strengths:

- You have had a lot of experience dealing with people.
- You have knowledge in your area of expertise.
- You've had the opportunity to work in another profession, but you have chosen to become a teacher because you feel it is a higher calling.
- You've worked with children in other capacities through the years, perhaps as a parent, coach, Sunday-school teacher, camp leader, or mentor.

From the get-go, as you survey school districts and prepare your cover letter and resume, have a positive, can-do attitude. Keep in mind that you're exactly what they're looking for, and you have much in your favor over the young, newly graduated teacher candidates.

In Your Cover Letter

Use the cover letter template and example in chapter 3 as guides when writing your letters. As a nontraditional applicant, here are the general requirements for the four paragraphs of your cover letter:

- **First paragraph:** This should be short and specific, naming the position for which you are applying.

- **Second paragraph:** This will be the longest paragraph in your cover letter. It should bubble with enthusiasm as you explain how your strengths and skills can help the school fulfill its needs. You can shine as you speak briefly of your life experiences, transferable skills, and subject knowledge. Let the reader know that you're familiar with the school and the district, and explain why you feel you will fit in with their philosophy.

- **Third paragraph:** Use this paragraph to explain your particular circumstances, why you have been out of teaching for a number of years, or why you have decided to switch careers at this time in your life.

- **Fourth paragraph:** Here is where you must win the reader's heart by convincing him or her of your passion for teaching. Also, thank the reader for considering you for the position, and request an interview.

You must make three *crucial* points in this cover letter:

- Your qualification for the position based on your life experiences and transferable skills

- Your knowledge of the school and the district

- Your passion for teaching

And remember these tips from chapter 3:

1. Your cover letter should be printed on high-quality plain white paper. Use a 12-point font, and do not exceed one page.

2. Use a formal business-style format for your letter—don't be too casual or overly friendly. Do not use contractions.

3. Check and double-check for typos, misspelled words, and grammatical errors. If possible, have someone proofread your letter.

On Your Resume

The strength of your resume will again be your life experiences, transferable skills, and many talents. Use the resumes shown in chapter 3 as examples (there are examples specifically for career switchers). Of course, the emphasis should be on your experiences, skills, and talents.

During the Interview

During your interview, as with your cover letter, be prepared to convince the hiring panel of your skills, your knowledge of the school, and your passion for teaching. By the way, when it comes to knowledge of the district, be aware of any innovative programs unique to the district, plus its goals and philosophy. Information about its programs is readily available on school report cards and brochures (see chapter 2).

The panel will want to know your reasons for changing careers and why you chose the field of classroom teaching. Be prepared to give them an honest, straightforward response. Within this response, convince them that the intangible quality of *passion* is clearly your motivating force for wanting to become a teacher. Explain that your decision was not impulsive or rash, and that much time and consideration went into your decision. Most panels will be impressed that you've made this gutsy move and will, with your help, see the advantages in hiring you.

> 24 percent of newly hired teachers in a recent year were career switchers.
> —National Center for Education Statistics

Sell yourself as an invaluable *product*. We have been on both sides of the table, and we know how this works!

Career-Switcher Success Stories

There's nothing quite like a success story to inspire you, so we've included a few for you here.

Patrick from Silicon Valley

When Patrick was laid off from his job as a marketing executive at a software company, he decided to do something he'd always wanted to do—become a teacher. It took him less than a month to find a job teaching computer science at a middle school in San Jose, California. He loves his new profession, even though it pays about half what his marketing position paid. He also must attend summer and evening classes for the next couple of years to qualify for a teaching certificate. He says this is the hardest thing he's ever tried to do, but the sense of satisfaction is great.

Nanette from Los Angeles

Nanette had spent 18 years in the fashion industry when, at the age of 46, she decided to enter the teaching profession. Although she knows she's overworked and underpaid, she refuses to give up her beloved fifth graders. She took her first graduate education course in the spring of 1998, and a year later she signed up as a fifth-grade teacher. Several other new teachers in her school have switched careers. One used to be an actor, and another was a personnel manager. She says they are people just like her who've "been there, done that" and now want a career that makes them proud to look in the mirror.

James from New York

At age 50, James has become an inner-city high school math teacher. In his previous professions he was a successful lawyer and criminal-court judge. After decades in these professions, he now feels free to finally step down from the bench and dive back into the subjects he loved most in college: math and physics. James got the idea when he answered an ad in the *New York Times,* in lettering that resembled a childish scrawl, that challenged readers to sign up for the most important job in New York City. He and 349 other job switchers attended a pep rally orientation for New York Fellows, an accelerated certification program started by schools chancellor Harold Levy. James' salary went from $125,600 as a New York City judge to $40,180 as a high school math teacher in Harlem. However, in spite of his pay cut, he says he's fulfilling what he describes as an even higher calling than that of a judge.

Brent from Tucson

Brent graduated from the accelerated one-year Teach for Tucson program offered by the University of Arizona. He's the quintessential example of a career switcher who is using the experiences of his previous career to advantage in his classroom. On his first day as a teacher, he offered his math students some inside information about his former job as an outdoor equipment sales representative. He worked up a practical mini-lesson using the retail cost of the kids' backpacks compared to their wholesale prices. Brent used the difference between retail and wholesale costs to teach the students how to calculate percentages. He feels that everything he teaches should have a context and should be relevant. Brent had 85 students in the first four classes he taught and had all their names memorized by his second week of teaching. He also has an interesting philosophy about

how a teacher should dress in the classroom. Although he dressed quite casually when he ran his business, he now wears a tie every day because he wants the kids to see that he takes their education seriously.

Part 2

INTERVIEWING FOR TEACHING JOBS

CHAPTER 6

Preparing for the Interview

The first step of preparing for an interview is knowing as much as you can about the schools and the surrounding community where you're interviewing. This knowledge serves two purposes: It helps you determine whether you really want to work in a given school or community, and it gives you an advantage during the interview.

These are important considerations. The former can keep you from accepting a job you'll hate. The latter gives you an edge over other candidates. Interview committees are impressed by candidates who take the time to research their schools and communities. It shows that you're willing to put in extra effort and that you're genuinely interested *in them.* Conversely, they'll know very quickly if you've just popped in and you don't have a clue about them or their district.

This chapter also clues you in to the top 21 questions that you will probably be asked at your interview. You need to think ahead of time how you will answer them. You can also rehearse your answers and practice role-playing, possibly with the help of a support group of other teacher candidates, as discussed later in this chapter. And finally, when you think you've got it all together, you can videotape yourself in a mock interview and see how you will come across to the interview panel. What you see might surprise you.

Do Your Homework

There are many places to find out the information you need before your interview. You should research and visit the community, the school district, and the individual school. The following sections give you tips on the most effective ways to conduct this research.

Research the Community

There are several ways to become familiar with a community. If you can visit the prospective community, this task becomes much easier.

If the school is located in a city, try to determine its attendance area (the area from which the school draws its students). In the case of elementary schools (grades K through 6), the area probably will be relatively small. Typically, urban elementary pupils live within one to two miles of their schools. A middle school or junior high school (grades 6 through 8 or 7 through 9) might serve the graduates of many elementary schools, making its attendance area much larger. Finally, a senior high (grades 9 or 10 through 12) might serve the graduates of one or two junior high schools. Sometimes, in fact, a rather large city will have only one high school.

If the school is located in a rural area, it might have a large attendance area covering many miles. In such situations, there might be only one elementary school and one high school serving pupils living 10 or more miles in all directions.

After you've determined the attendance area, drive, bicycle, or walk through it. Talk with people or students you meet. Are they friendly and helpful? Ask how youth-oriented the community is. Does it provide parks, recreational facilities, and programs for young people? Note the community's general appearance. Are the houses and yards reasonably neat and clean? If you meet someone who really impresses you, try to remember his or her name.

Spend half a day wandering around the area, and you'll get a good feel for the community. It will be warm, friendly, and trusting; cold, unfriendly, and suspicious; or something in between. By the end of your tour you'll probably have a definite opinion about the community and its residents.

If you're unable to visit the community before the interview, you can still find out something about it by contacting the Chamber of Commerce and requesting relevant information. If there is no Chamber of Commerce, try the local Visitors' Bureau or subscribe to a local newspaper or read it online for a month. Of course, one of the best sources of information is the city or town's Web

> Of the teacher candidates in our survey, 49 percent said they had researched the communities where they were scheduled to be interviewed.

site, if one exists. Although these sources won't substitute for actually being there, they can provide worthwhile information.

In chapter 2 we talked about doing school surveys as part of your research for finding job openings. Although the research you do here is similar, there's one big difference: The school surveys were part of your general job search strategy; the research you're doing now is to prepare you for a scheduled interview for a specific position. Your motivation for researching the community takes on a new, and more exciting, meaning.

Research the School District

In addition to researching the community, you should research the school district and the particular school where you'll be working if you are hired.

There are many sources of information on schools and school districts:

- You should start with the *state schools directory* for your state. This resource is available in your college library or placement office. It lists each county office of education for the state and the districts and schools within each county or parish, along with each

Of the teacher candidates in our survey, 21 percent tried to learn as much as possible about the policies of the school district where they were scheduled to be interviewed.

  school's address, telephone number, size, grades taught, and administrators.

- Another source is the *county schools directory,* which includes more detailed information, such as each school's staff and grade assignments.

- Access the *school district's Web site,* which should include specific information about each of the schools within the district. You can also read a specific school's report card by accessing the Web site of your state's board of education (see the appendix) and then clicking the link to school report cards. These report cards contain a brief description of the school, including its location, the community it serves, its size, grades taught, ethnicity, and other interesting information (see the following list).

  To locate the school district's Web site, go to your favorite search engine and type the name of the district. The district's Web site should be at the top of the list of finds.

- Finally, the most comprehensive source of information on a particular school is the *school's directory* or handbook, which is available at the school itself.

When you've gathered all these resources, you'll have the information you need about a given school or district.

Here are some other items often included in a school report card:

- Student attendance
- Amount of money spent per student
- Type of textbooks used
- Salary information
- Current training and curriculum projects
- Leadership provided

- Results of student achievement tests
- Description of the facilities
- Classroom discipline and climate for learning
- Teacher evaluation policy
- Student support services offered

These reports provide useful information for comparing one school to another.

Visit the School

Finally, the ultimate school research opportunity is a visit to an individual school campus. Most administrators welcome nonintrusive visits from teacher candidates. Notice that we said "nonintrusive." Keep in mind that the school's primary function is to educate students, so your visit should interfere as little as possible with that function.

Call the school in advance, and explain why you'd like to visit. Your evaluation of the school begins with this phone call. Chances are you'll talk with the school secretary—usually a school's "initial image." How are you received? How efficiently does the person deal with your request?

Assuming you're given permission to visit, be sure to show up on time. You should dress appropriately—as if you were coming for an interview: no shorts or tank tops, no scuffed athletic shoes *sans* socks. You get the idea.

"Interviewers appreciate an interviewee who is prepared."
—Max Eggert in *The Perfect Interview*

As you drive up to the campus, check out its general appearance. Are the grounds free of litter? Does the landscaping look good?

Next, check out the building. Is the paint in good condition? Is there litter or graffiti? Are the windows and doors clean? The building's age shouldn't affect the learning going on inside its walls. In fact, an old building that's clean and well-maintained almost always houses an educational program superior to that of a newer building that's dirty and poorly maintained. A school's physical appearance speaks volumes about its students, staff, and program.

As you enter the building, what do you see? Are signs posted giving clear directions to the office, or are you greeted with blank walls and left to figure it out for yourself? Go to the office immediately, by the way, because administrators don't like strangers wandering around the campus.

As you enter the office, are you met with a warm greeting and a smile? Or do you feel like you're entering a war zone? Do you sense a cold "What do you want? Can't you see we're busy here?" attitude? In most cases, you'll be received with a warm greeting. School secretaries, we've found, are almost always friendly and helpful.

At this time you'll be given directions for your visit. You might have an opportunity to visit briefly with the principal, or the secretary might direct you to a particular classroom. If you visit a classroom, the general rule is to enter without knocking. If the teacher is presenting a lesson or working with a group of students, move to the back of the room, and wait for the teacher to come to you. If the teacher is not occupied with students when you enter, approach him or her and introduce yourself. The teacher will then tell you where to sit during your observation. It's usually best to observe from the rear of the classroom so that you don't distract the students.

> "Talking to teachers in the district (where I was to be interviewed) got me headed in the right direction."
> —Middle-school science teacher in North Dakota

Try to talk with any staff members you meet during your visit; they'll help you form an opinion of the school. Visit the playground and the staff room during breaks and the student dining area and faculty lounge during lunch.

If you spend only three hours on the campus (say, from 10 a.m. to 1 p.m.), you won't know everything about the school, but you'll know considerably more than most candidates for the position.

Before leaving the campus, check back at the office and thank those responsible for your visit. You might also send a thank-you note later that day. This is a classy touch that makes you stand out from other candidates.

> Be agreeable and flexible when scheduling your interviews. If you are offered a certain time slot for your interview, try to make it work. If the time slot is impossible for you, don't suggest another specific day and time, but give the scheduler general time spans when you will be available—"any time Tuesday or Thursday morning," and so forth. Then, let the scheduler suggest actual time slots for you to consider.

Taking time to research a community and its schools won't assure you a job; however, it will enhance your chances of being offered a contract—and it just might keep you from signing a contract you will regret later.

Network with Other Teacher Candidates

In chapter 2, we discussed networking as a process of making contacts and establishing relationships as part of the job search. The kind of networking we're talking about here is the same concept, but on a much smaller scale. It involves forming a network of a half-dozen or so of your teacher-candidate friends. This cozy little group, in effect, becomes a support group as much as a networking team, so it's important to find people who share some basic qualities with you:

- They have a sense of humor.
- They're seeking jobs close to the same grade level.
- They share common ideas about the job search.
- They buy into the philosophy of small-group networking.

Although it's best to have at least five or six members, if you can find only three or four who meet the criteria, go ahead and form a group. The group's closeness and compatibility are more important than the number of members.

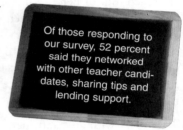

Of those responding to our survey, 52 percent said they networked with other teacher candidates, sharing tips and lending support.

Here are some ways you and the members of your network group can be helpful to one another:

- You can share ideas and information about job leads and job search tips.
- You can give and receive advice and constructive criticism. (Remember, this should always be done in a positive way.)
- You can encourage each other as much as possible.
- You can do mock interviews and role-playing and respond to hypotheticals and possible interview questions. (You'll read more about these later in this chapter.)
- You can discuss strategies of the interview process:
    - *Questions you should ask during the interview*
    - *Questions you should avoid during the interview*
    - *Body language*
    - *Social skills*
    - *Voice, grooming, and attire*
    - *Attitude*

As members of the group sign teaching contracts, they should be encouraged to stay with the group as long as they can, offering support, encouragement, and constructive criticism, especially during mock interviews.

"Networking with other teacher candidates led me to pursue job openings of which I was originally unaware."
—Secondary social studies teacher in New Jersey

One note of caution regarding these networking groups: Remember that your small support group is only one part of your total networking effort. Don't let your cozy little group become so warm and comfortable that you neglect your other job search efforts.

Later, we'll talk about a couple ways to put your group to work—specifically, as you prepare for the interview. You'll find suggestions for using a video camera during your meetings, which will boost your confidence when it comes time for real interviews. You'll also see why we listed "a sense of humor" as a necessity for each member of the group. It should be fun, so read on.

Prepare Responses to Possible Interview Questions

When you walk into an interview room, you'll have about 30 minutes to sell yourself. During this brief time you might be asked only eight or ten questions. Your responses to these questions are crucial. Because you don't know which questions will be asked, you need to be prepared for anything.

The fact that you were called for an interview—that you made the paper cut—means that they like you so far. Now it's up to you to impress them with your excellent responses to their questions. Your responses should be clear and concise; don't ramble. Make your point and go on! If you're asked a straightforward question, give a straightforward answer. On the other hand, if you're asked an open-ended question, always take it as a valuable opportunity to tell the interview panel what you want them to know. This might be a good time to work in some of your special skills and talents or to share something from your portfolio. Sell yourself!

As we gathered information for this book, we asked interviewers what questions they typically ask at the interview table. We also asked newly hired teachers what questions they were asked during their interviews. We combined these two lists, discarded any questions that related to isolated situations, and grouped the remaining questions into two categories: the top 21 questions asked during interviews, and other frequently asked questions.

The Top 21 Questions Asked During Interviews

Be prepared to respond to these questions, because you'll undoubtedly hear many of them during your interviews. Practice your responses with a friend or in front of your networking group. Ask for their constructive criticism of your answers, and then polish your performance until you can respond in a natural way without hesitation.

We have given you some help on this list of questions by offering comments about *What They're Really Asking* and *Tips* to help you prepare.

1. What is your greatest strength as a teacher?

What They're Really Asking
- How do you perceive your talents and abilities as a teacher?
- Will you be an asset to our school and our students?

Tips
- They're crying for you to sell yourself here; don't let them down.
- Have six or seven responses memorized.
- Don't blow smoke.
- Be "confidently humble."

2. What is your greatest weakness?

What They're Really Asking
- How honest are you being with us and with yourself?
- How realistic are you?
- What skeletons do you have in your "teaching closet" that we should know about?

Tips
- Review the section in chapter 1 on ways to present a weakness as a positive.
- Don't sell yourself down the river with your response.

3. Tell us about yourself.

What They're Really Asking

- What makes you special?
- Why should we hire you?
- How organized and concise are you?
- How confident are you?
- What qualities might you bring to our children?
- Who are you? Do we want you to work with our children?

Tips

- Have several powerful selling points ready for this one.
- Give a brief, concise response in less than two minutes.
- Use most of your response time selling yourself.
- This is an open-ended question, a chance for you to impress them.
- This is no time for humility, but don't step over the line of arrogance, either.

4. What is your philosophy of classroom discipline?

What They're Really Asking

- Do you *have* a plan?
- How will you implement your plan?
- Do you think this is important?
- Can you control kids?

Tips

- Be ready to give an example of a discipline "ladder" or plan.
- Be prepared to tell why you like it, and give examples of how it's worked for you.
- Discipline is one of the most important areas of concern in schools today. Handle this subject well!

5. What steps would you take with a student who is disruptive in your classroom?

What They're Really Asking

- Do you have a classroom discipline plan?
- Can you handle most discipline problems yourself, or will you send students to the principal's office at the drop of a hat?
- What is your general philosophy of classroom discipline?

Tips

- This question is similar to question 4; be ready to describe a discipline plan and how you will implement it.
- Reaffirm your philosophy of discipline.
- Again, the subject of classroom discipline is a major concern for most hiring panels.

6. What kind of classroom-management plan do you like best? How would you implement it in your classroom?

What They're Really Asking

- If we walk into your classroom, what will we see going on?
- How will your lessons be planned?
- Will your students stay on task and be challenged?

Tips

- You need to explain your management plan briefly, completely, and in an organized way.
- Interview committees are not looking for a morgue setting, nor do they want a three-ring circus. They're looking for an intellectually stimulating, organized, respectful environment in which students do well academically and socially.
- Explain how you'll implement your plan in terms of behavior; recall your teacher-education classes and your student-teaching experiences.
- You'll almost certainly be asked a question similar to this, because it's an area of critical importance in most school districts.

7. Why do you want to be a teacher?

What They're Really Asking

- How dedicated are you?
- Do you have a passion for children and the teaching profession?
- How will our children benefit by having you as their teacher?

Tips

- If you have a passion for kids, this one should be easy. Don't get carried away, though; keep it simple and to the point.
- Stay away from a response like "Most of my family members have been teachers." This won't get you very far.

8. Why do you want to teach in this district/school?

What They're Really Asking

- Do you care where you teach?
- Did you take the time to research our district/school?
- Are you right for our schools and our children?

Tips

- This is a great PR question. If your school survey put this district high on your list, the answer will come easily. Without overdoing it, tell them how great they are!
- Tell them that you *do* want to work for them!

9. Why should we hire you?

What They're Really Asking

- Can you convince us that you're the one?
- Can you sell your "product?"
- How much confidence do you have in yourself?

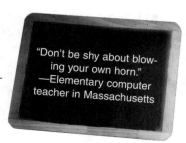

"Don't be shy about blowing your own horn."
—Elementary computer teacher in Massachusetts

Tips

- Be ready to make a powerful statement of your value to the school or district.
- This is no time for humility, but don't be arrogant, either.

10. What are your goals in education? Where do you see yourself five years from now? How does this position fit into your career plans?

What They're Really Asking

- Do you want to stay in one position for the long haul, or will you be here only a year before moving on?
- Are you a stable person?
- Have you set goals for yourself?
- Have you given any thought to your future?

Tips

- They want another perspective on you.
- They might not want to hire someone who will be moving on in a year or two.
- There's nothing wrong with simply saying that you have one goal in mind right now, and that is to become the best teacher possible.

11. What would we see if we walked into your classroom?

What They're Really Asking

- What is your philosophy of education?
- What kind of teacher are you?
- Do you have a well-managed classroom?
- Do your students interact with you and each other?

Tips

- This is a good time for name-dropping. Show off your knowledge of new and proven methods and trends (for example, grouping of students, cooperative learning, and use of manipulatives and hands-on teaching materials).
- You might say: "You would see the students arranged in groups; a pleasant atmosphere; a room that is comfortable and pleasing to the eye; students who are under control, yet busy, with a healthy amount of noise going on; children learning in different modalities: visual, auditory, and kinesthetic."
- Avoid the tendency to go into too much detail. They might be interested in how you'll arrange the students' desks, but they don't really want to know what's inside each desk.

12. What are some trends, issues, and methodologies in education that relate to your specific curriculum area or grade level?

What They're Really Asking

- Do you know what's going on in education today?
- Do you have a passion for the profession of teaching?

Tips

- Read educational journals and periodicals regularly.
- Familiarize yourself with current trends and buzzwords in education.
- Talk with your peers and other educators in your field.
- Visit schools as often as you can to observe the latest teaching methods.
- Join a professional organization.

13. What book are you currently reading or have you read recently?

What They're Really Asking

- Teachers should be avid readers; are you a reader?
- What are your interests?
- How well-rounded are you?

Tips

- This question is often asked, so be ready for it.
- If you've lost the recreational reading "bug" because of your hectic schedule, take some time to read a variety of fiction, nonfiction, and professional books.

14. What are some of your hobbies or leisure-time activities?

What They're Really Asking

- How well-rounded are you?
- What do you do outside of school that will transfer positively into the classroom?

Tips

- Here's another opportunity to sell yourself; take advantage of questions like these.
- Emphasize any of your hobbies or leisure-time activities that could carry over to your classroom.
- The interview committee is trying to find out more about you, and they know your life outside the classroom can tell them a lot. So don't just *answer* questions; *respond* to them.

15. What special skills or talents will you bring to your classroom?

What They're Really Asking

- How well-rounded are you?
- Do you have a wide variety of interests and experiences that will make you an exciting, stimulating teacher?

Tips

- This is your time to shine!
- Be prepared to state in an organized, succinct fashion any skills or talents you'll bring to their school, but be careful that you don't overdo it.

16. How would you involve the community in your classroom?

What They're Really Asking

- Are you willing to reach out and seek community expertise?

Tips

- Be familiar with this concept.
- Be prepared to give examples of community members visiting the classroom, as well as local field trips you might have taken.

17. Would you be willing to teach at a different grade level (elementary) or teach a different subject (secondary)?

What They're Really Asking

- Are you flexible?
- Do you have enough confidence to consider other grade levels or subject areas?
- How's your attitude?

Tips

- You need to think about this possibility in advance. The committee might have already found the right person for the advertised position, and now they're looking for someone who can adapt to their needs if another position becomes available. Administrators like to have options, and they're always looking for teachers who are flexible and versatile.
- A positive response here might give you a leg up on your competition!

18. Would you be willing to pursue an extra certificate or credential?

What They're Really Asking

- How is your attitude?
- How flexible are you?
- Are you a teacher who will increase our staffing options?

Tips

- School districts frequently are required to employ teachers who have special credentials or certificates to qualify for special program funds. If you have certain specialized credentials or certificates in addition to your basic teaching credential, you become more valuable to the district.
- If all things are equal, the position will go to the candidate who is willing to pursue one of these "extras."
- This is a perfect time to tell the hiring panel how important professional growth is to you.

19. What is your philosophy of team teaching?

What They're Really Asking

- Are you flexible?
- Do you work well with others?
- Do you have experience in team teaching?
- Do you know anything about the methodology of team teaching?

Tips

- Be prepared to talk about this concept in a favorable way.
- Share a few positive points in favor of team teaching, such as these:
  - *Team teaching is a powerful and efficient method for dealing with a large number of students.*
  - *It's very effective for teachers to work together and share their ideas.*
  - *You might say, "I haven't had the opportunity to be involved in a teaming situation yet, but I understand it can result in more efficient use of time in the classroom." Or, "If teachers at my grade level have determined that team teaching would better the learning process of our students, I'm very willing to try it. I enjoy working and sharing with other teachers, and I want the best for our kids."*

20. What were you hoping we would ask you today, but didn't?

What They're Really Asking

- Is there anything special about yourself that you want us to know?

Tips

- Speak up—sell yourself.
- This is a great opportunity to "show and tell" one more time, using materials from your portfolio to convince them how valuable you'll be to their district. Go for it!

21. Do you have any questions for us?

What They're Really Asking

- Are you interested enough in our district to ask questions?
- How prepared are you to ask questions?
- Have you given this some thought?

Tips

- See "Questions You Should Ask" in chapter 8.

- Be sure you have at least one question ready to ask, or have five or six listed on a 3 × 5 card. The panel will be impressed that you came prepared.

- *Never* say, "No, you've answered all my questions."

Other Questions

Read through this list of questions and decide how you'll respond to each one in an interview. Ask yourself, "What are they really asking?"

22. At what point do you involve the principal in a discipline matter?

23. How would you describe the ideal teacher?

24. What are your plans for professional growth?

25. If you were hired to teach starting this year, how would you go about setting up your reading program?

26. Do you prefer homogeneous or heterogeneous grouping? Why?

27. In which curriculum areas do you feel particularly strong?

28. Would you be willing to coach a sport, advise an organization, or assist with extracurricular activities?

29. What experience do you have with this age group?

30. Do you see yourself as a "team player?"

31. How would you motivate a student who won't even try?

32. Describe a time when a lesson was not going well; what did you do about it?

33. How would you compare the whole-language approach to reading to a phonics-based approach?

34. How would you implement cooperative grouping in your classroom?

35. What are some ways you would communicate with a parent regarding a student's progress?

36. While in high school and college, in which extracurricular activities did you participate? Did you hold an office?

37. How would you integrate language arts across the curriculum?

38. What community projects or organizations have you been involved with?

39. How would your best friend describe you?

> "The most important thing is that teacher candidates really know their subject areas."
> —Member of a panel who interviews teachers on the secondary level in Florida

40. Who are some people who have had a great impact on your life?

41. What would you like to share about your student-teaching experience?

42. Which critical skills do you think are required to be a successful teacher?

43. How do you involve parents in your classroom?

44. What kind of principal would you like to work for?

45. What do you know about our school district?

46. How do you go about deciding what should be taught in your classroom?

47. What gives you the greatest pleasure in teaching?

48. What is your philosophy and practice of the teacher's role as a member of the school staff?

49. How would you go about grouping your students in mathematics?

50. What does individualized instruction mean to you?

51. Which evaluation techniques or testing procedures would you use to determine student academic growth?

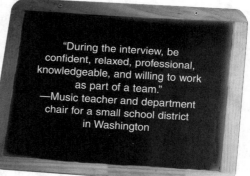

"During the interview, be confident, relaxed, professional, knowledgeable, and willing to work as part of a team."
—Music teacher and department chair for a small school district in Washington

52. How effective is it to call parents for a conference when a problem has developed with their son or daughter?

53. Describe a belief you hold about education. How would you implement it in the classroom?

54. What are some of the new teaching textbooks and materials being used in your grade level or subject area?

55. What is your philosophy regarding the Thematic Approach in teaching the curriculum?

56. At which grade level do you feel you would do the best job?

57. Have you had any background in designing lesson plans with behavioral objectives in your teaching? How do you feel about them?

58. Are there any undesirable things about teaching that you can think of?

59. What is the worst thing that ever happened to you in the classroom?

60. Do you feel your job as a teacher goes beyond the three-o'clock bell? How?

61. How much time, if any, would you be able to spend working on after-school projects or programs?

62. How would you expect your principal to help you?

63. How would you handle varied reading abilities in the content areas?

64. An experienced teacher offers you the following advice: "Be sure to command the respect of your students immediately, and everything will go well." How do you feel about this?

65. What would you say to a parent who complains that your teaching is irrelevant to his or her child's needs?

66. What would you do with a student who is obviously gifted or talented in a particular area?

67. What are some ways a student can show mastery of a concept?

68. What is meant by Diagnostic and Prescriptive Learning?

69. What are negative consequences and positive reinforcement, and the effects of each?

70. What steps would you take to turn a habitually tardy student into a punctual student?

71. How do you motivate students to develop self-discipline?

72. What are some ways to let parents know about the positive things going on in your classroom?

73. What would you tell a parent who complains that you don't give his or her child enough homework?

74. If we asked your closest teaching associate to tell us how well you get along with children and adults, what would that person say?

75. How did you choose your college major?

76. What kind of relationship should teachers develop with their students?

77. How would you establish and maintain positive relationships with students, parents, staff, and others in the community?

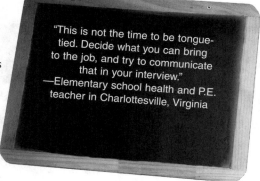

"This is not the time to be tongue-tied. Decide what you can bring to the job, and try to communicate that in your interview."
—Elementary school health and P.E. teacher in Charlottesville, Virginia

78. What do you understand the Inquiry Method to be in the areas of science and social science?

79. What is your attitude toward Individual versus Total Class discipline?

80. What do you think is wrong with education today? What is right?

81. If students constantly complained to you about another teacher, what would you do?

82. What professional association meetings have you attended within the past year?

83. How would you teach Critical Thinking to your students?

84. How would you use Authentic Assessment?

A Few Final Words of Advice

Here are a few final general tips to keep in mind while interviewing:

- Don't let your responses sound "canned" or rehearsed; pause before responding to a question, as if giving it serious thought.

- Keep your best skills and traits in mind as you respond to questions; be ready to work them into the dialogue in a natural way.

- If you're a new teacher and you can't respond to some of the panel's questions based on past classroom experience, emphasize your many job-related skills that can be transferred to the classroom. Also let the panel see your enthusiasm, motivation, and passion for children and for the teaching profession.

A Word About Coaching

Many teacher candidates in our survey reported being asked whether they would be willing to coach a sport in addition to teaching their regular classes. Coaching isn't for everyone, obviously, but if you have an interest in athletics in general, or in one sport in particular, you should definitely consider pursuing this "extra" for these reasons:

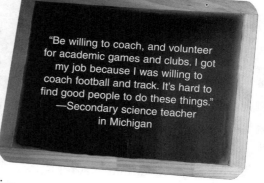

"Be willing to coach, and volunteer for academic games and clubs. I got my job because I was willing to coach football and track. It's hard to find good people to do these things."
—Secondary science teacher in Michigan

- If the district needs someone to coach a sport in addition to teaching a regular single-subject curriculum, this could very well land you the position. This is especially true in smaller schools.

- Ordinarily you are compensated for your coaching. An extra $1,500 to $2,000 each year could be very attractive.

- Coaching can create special contacts with kids. Most coaches agree that the coach/athlete relationship can be powerful and can help you make a life-long, positive impact on a young person's life. Stepping out of your role in the classroom and onto the playing field can break down barriers that inhibit a child's trust of you.

- Coaching can be, and often is, a lot of fun. We have spent many hours after school in the gym or on the playing field. If you're considering coaching as one more way to market yourself, don't overlook the "fun factor."

Rehearse Role-Playing and Hypotheticals

First, let's look at the difference between role-playing and hypotheticals. With a hypothetical, you must explain how you would handle a given scenario the panel has set up for you. Here's an example: "How would you deal with an angry parent who comes into your classroom during a class session and demands your immediate attention?"

With role-playing, you assume the role of the teacher, and the interview panel plays the "devil's advocate," such as a group of parents who want to confront you over a particular issue. For example, you, as the teacher, must defend your position on whole language versus phonics-based reading. The hiring panel takes the position of the parent group that opposes your view. This is playacting, and it takes most people out of their comfort zone. For this reason, it's important to rehearse role-playing with your friends. Our survey shows that it's not often required during an interview, but it does happen, so you need to be prepared.

As you practice role-playing and responding to hypotheticals, you need to picture possible interview settings. One setting would be a one-on-one interview in which the principal sits behind a desk and you sit directly in front of it. If an interview panel is conducting the interview, panel members usually sit at a large table, and you sit at a desk or a smaller table 10 to 15 feet in front of them.

Of the teacher candidates in our survey, 38 percent reported being asked to role-play or respond to hypotheticals during an interview, but only 20 percent of them had rehearsed ahead of time.

The atmosphere of the interview can be formal or informal, depending on the administrator or the makeup of the interview team. Most interviewers try to promote a relaxed atmosphere in the hope that you'll feel free to be yourself so that they can see the "real you."

It's natural to be a little nervous during an interview, but to this we say, "Trust us." We can't think of a single interview we've been involved in that was an unpleasant experience. So as you prepare for your interviews, remember to relax, be yourself, and enjoy the experience. Try to have a positive mind-set as you practice role-playing and responding to hypotheticals.

Some Common Hypotheticals and Role-Playing Scenarios

Here are some of the most common hypotheticals or role-playing scenarios presented during interviews. You'd be asked to respond to each scenario:

- One of your students becomes disruptive.
- A student reveals some very personal concerns but then withdraws and says nothing further.
- One of your students becomes violent.
- A parent becomes very angry during a parent-teacher conference.
- One of your students doesn't respond to your discipline plan.
- Take a position on whole language or phonics, and defend it.
- You suspect that a project turned in by a student was completed by someone else.
- After you give an assignment, you notice a student quietly crying.
- Two of your students are fighting.
- A student refuses to salute the flag or observe certain holidays.
- You observe a student cheating on a test.
- A student reveals a situation at home that makes you think she may be the victim of some kind of abuse.
- You disagree with your principal's method of handling a given situation.
- One of your students becomes belligerent and defies you.
- A student brings you some money, says he found it, and asks if he can keep it.
- You feel your principal is not supporting you in a difficult situation.
- A student has an accident on the playground; he's on the ground and unable to move.

This is by no means a complete list of the scenarios you may encounter during an interview. One thing you can count on, however, is that a significant number of scenarios will involve either a confrontational situation with a parent or a discipline/behavior problem with a student.

Tip: It's obvious that school districts place a tremendous emphasis on discipline and classroom management. And you can understand why. They want to feel confident that you, as a new teacher, have a good, sound, fair method of class management. You can't wimp out in this area. So, before you go into the interview, be sure you have a specific discipline plan in mind. Review what you learned in your teacher training courses and from your reading. You may also want to consider the solid, practical ideas in our first book, _The Unauthorized Teacher's Survival Guide._ In chapter 7 of that book, we suggest many discipline methods and ideas of our own, as well as those of experts in the field.

Practicing with Your Networking Group

As we discussed earlier, it's helpful to network with other teacher candidates as you prepare for interviews. It's especially helpful to rehearse your role-playing and responses to hypotheticals with this group. Members of the group can tell what scenarios have been presented during their past interviews, and the group can reenact them during your networking time together.

It's also a good idea for someone in your networking group to throw in a real ringer once in a while, such as this one, which was actually asked of one of our survey participants:

Billie is passing around pamphlets denying the Holocaust. What do you do?

Wow! What _do_ you do? We remember when the toughies were something like "Suzie has an eraser stuck up her nose" or "Jason threw up in the back of the bus."

If you're asked a really sticky question (like the preceding one about the Holocaust), you can always tell the hiring panel that you would seek the advice of your site administrator. And if the interview committee throws you a very difficult hypothetical, remember that there could be several appropriate responses, and what they might _really_ want to know is how you think and react on the spot.

That's why it's so important for you to practice role-playing and reacting to hypotheticals _before_ your first interview.

> **Tip:** Whenever possible, answer a hypothetical question with a real-life example of how you successfully handled the problem in the past. This concept is based on the CAR principle (challenge - action - result) and is being incorporated into interviews in the corporate world. It's always stronger to tell how you *handled* or *solved* a certain problem in the past, as opposed to explaining how you *would* handle it if it happens in the future.

Videotape Mock Interviews

Now that you've prepared your responses to interview questions and practiced role-playing and responding to hypotheticals, it's time to videotape a mock interview. You will find this to be the most valuable thing you can do in preparation for the real thing.

Get together with some of your networking buddies, and find a private room where you can get down to the serious business of videotaping one another. We know this is an intimidating exercise for some people, but—trust us on this one—you'll be rewarded at the interview table. Participating in mock interviews, especially if you can see yourself on videotape, will improve your confidence level, your use of body language, your voice level and speech patterns, and your ability to articulate responses clearly and concisely.

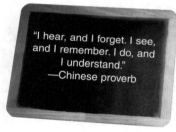

"I hear, and I forget. I see, and I remember. I do, and I understand."
—Chinese proverb

The Rules

Here are the ground rules:

- You need a video camera, plus one videotape *per person.*
- Take turns being "it" while the rest of the group plays the part of the interview panel, asking questions and presenting hypothetical scenarios for you to respond to.
- After each candidate's performance, replay the tape, and immediately participate in an open, honest, *constructive* critique. Make notes of the problem areas you want to work on before your next videotaping session.
- Take turns until you've all had your 15 minutes of fame.
- Schedule another group taping session as soon as possible, preferably within two weeks.

- Take your tape with you so that you can watch your performance once more in the privacy of your home. Study the tape carefully, and work on your flaws before the next session.

Schedule a third and final taping session to which everyone wears their interview attire. By this time you'll be familiar with our tips for sharpening your personal appeal (listed in chapter 7) and will be able to share some helpful advice. This final session is a good time to present a mini-lesson in front of the camera. Although only 6 percent of the teacher candidates in our survey said they were asked to plan or present an impromptu mini-lesson during an interview, it doesn't hurt to be prepared, just in case.

Have fun with these mock interviews. Be prepared to laugh and be laughed at in a good-natured way. When we first discussed these networking groups earlier in the chapter, you might recall that a sense of humor was listed as a necessary attribute for every member; now you know why. There's no way to get through these mock interview sessions without cracking up at some point, but it's all part of the experience.

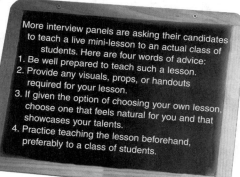

More interview panels are asking their candidates to teach a live mini-lesson to an actual class of students. Here are four words of advice:
1. Be well prepared to teach such a lesson.
2. Provide any visuals, props, or handouts required for your lesson.
3. If given the option of choosing your own lesson, choose one that feels natural for you and that showcases your talents.
4. Practice teaching the lesson beforehand, preferably to a class of students.

By the way, you might want to do two rounds of taping during the first session—a round of questions and responses followed by a round of role-playing and responding to hypotheticals. This way you won't constantly shift gears between the two interviewing styles.

It's Difficult, But Worth It

What is the value of all this? Why suffer through such an uncomfortable exercise? Because there's no way to really know how you come across during an interview until you see yourself on videotape. This means setting aside your pride and putting your ego on the line as you watch yourself make the mistakes we all make under the pressure of a camera and in front of our peers.

You might be surprised to see yourself as others see you: twisting your ring around and around on your finger as you speak, saying "you know" every other sentence, or crossing your arms when asked a question (a nonverbal, defensive sign that you resent the question or dislike the interviewer). However, by detecting these flaws ahead of time, you can make some changes: holding your hands still, not saying "you know," and replacing your negative, closed position with a warm, positive, open posture.

The value of these sessions is great, although you might not realize it until you get to the interview table, where you'll feel ready for just about anything. We realize, of course, that you might be asked a few questions that are worded differently than those listed in this chapter. But the underlying motives for the questions will be the same, and the confidence you gain through the mock interviews will be immeasurable.

And here's a special word of encouragement for you if you feel you don't interview well or you choke when you get to the interview table. You'll find that by participating in these mock interviews, your fears will dissipate substantially (although they probably won't disappear). Just remember that everyone who sits on a hiring panel expects to see a certain amount of nervousness from the candidates. For that matter, we've had several personnel directors, principals, and other members of interview committees tell us that *they* get nervous or uncomfortable when conducting an interview.

"Practice your interviews!"
—Member of an interview committee for a rural school district in Idaho

So, don't let the butterflies in your stomach make your head spin! By participating in mock interview sessions; accepting the friendly critique of your networking peers; and continuing to practice, practice, practice, you'll reduce those butterflies considerably and be able to walk into any job interview with confidence.

CHAPTER 7

Sharpening Your Personal Appeal

Your interviews are drawing near, and you're probably feeling pretty confident after all those mock interview sessions and role-playing rehearsals. That's good, because what you say during the interview is crucial. There's something else to consider, however, and that is what you *don't say*. This is known as the *silent language* or *subtext*. Subtext is a powerful force that can contradict what you say; likewise, it can reinforce your statements.

Your subtext is revealed through your posture, eye contact, subtle gestures, the sound of your voice, the rhythm of your speech, your handshake, your dress, your facial expressions, and your personal grooming. This silent language is so dynamic that it can actually alter the hiring panel's perception of you.

To give you a graphic illustration, observe any court trial, and you'll notice that the defense attorney has altered the defendant's subtext to sway the jury. If a man has been accused of rape, for example, you can be sure he will appear in court wearing a beautifully tailored, conservative business suit, a pressed white shirt, and a "sincere" tie. His hair will be cut and styled, his fingernails will be clean and trimmed, and his nose stud will be stuffed into one of his pockets. He'll also *appear* to be relaxed and confident, from his posture to his eye contact. The result of all this manipulation, his attorney hopes, is that at least one person on the jury will say, "He sure doesn't *look* like a rapist!"

In fact, many studies have concluded that any attractive, well-dressed defendant is favored by the jury because he or she is *perceived* as less likely to be guilty.

> You have only one chance to make a first impression.

Or consider the example of a girl who attended a large city high school. She ran with a gang of girls she called "punks," who all spiked their hair, wore blue lipstick, and pierced their tongues. None of them was doing well in school. The girl wondered whether her grades would improve if she changed her image, so she took some drastic measures. Not only did she do away with the hair spikes, blue lipstick, and tongue jewelry, but she toned down her wardrobe.

Bingo! Her grades began to improve. Her efforts changed her image not only in the eyes of her teachers, but in her own eyes as well. Smart girl!

Our purpose in this chapter is to make you aware of the subtle messages conveyed by your silent language, especially as they relate to your job interviews. You want members of hiring panels to like you at "first glance," from the moment you enter the room. Studies have shown, in fact, that your first impression is a lasting impression: How you are perceived during that first 10 seconds is what people remember!

Dress and Grooming

Men should dress conservatively, in a business suit or a coordinated sport jacket and slacks. You should always wear a tie, but nothing faddish or novel.

Women should wear a conservative suit or dress, preferably with a classic line. A dress or a blouse, jacket, and skirt are two good choices. Avoid anything that's too frilly, trendy, or "cute." Don't wear a pantsuit, because it might give the impression that you're not taking the interview seriously. (You'll have plenty of chances to wear them after you're hired.) Also, avoid miniskirts and blouses that are frilly, off-the-shoulder, or low-cut.

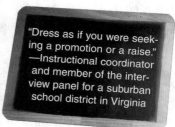

"Dress as if you were seeking a promotion or a raise."
—Instructional coordinator and member of the interview panel for a suburban school district in Virginia

Colors

Avoid bright colors or extremes. For men, dark blue and charcoal gray project a subtext of strength and competence. Black is considered too formal for a teaching interview, and you should avoid tan because it doesn't project confidence. Light gray is a possibility, depending on your coloring. A classic navy blazer with dark-gray slacks is always a safe choice.

Men's shirts should be white, light gray, or blue. The tie should be tastefully muted in stripes, small dots, or paisley. Be aware of your own coloring, and choose a tie that gives you a feeling of self-confidence.

If you wear suspenders, they should match the color of your tie (although they should be completely covered by your jacket).

The most important thing is that you select something that makes you feel good about yourself. If you feel good about yourself and you like the way you look, this image will be projected to the hiring panel.

Women can choose from a range of conservative colors. If you're undecided, you can't go wrong with navy blue. Feeling good about yourself is the most important factor, so try on several outfits before the interview, and then choose the one that creates the strongest self-image.

Teacher Dress Codes

Because some teachers around the country are beginning to "dress down" to the extreme, many school districts have recently established strict dress codes for their teachers. These districts want to stop the trend toward skimpy tops, short skirts, flip-flops, jeans, T-shirts, see-through blouses, spandex, and clothing that exposes "cleavage, private parts, the midriff, or undergarments." Be familiar with the dress code for the district for which you're being interviewed. Here are a few excerpts from recently adopted dress codes:

- "Abundant research exists to indicate that personal appearance has a significant effect upon other people. As public school employees, we are all employed in positions of influence. Our dress, grooming, and mannerisms will have an impact upon the way students and parents respond to our leadership."

  —Harris County Schools, Georgia

- "It is important that everyone continue to recognize that school is a more formal experience and the type of apparel worn should reflect that. Teachers are expected to set a good example for students and should not allow themselves to become careless in their grooming and attire."

  —Aldine Independent School District, Texas

- "The professional appearance...of staff members not only reinforces their own shared vision of the district and their identity as highly motivated professionals working toward a common mission, but also strengthens their morale, sense of professionalism, dignity, and self-worth."

  —Colorado Springs District 11, Colorado

- "It shall be the policy of the school board to require its employees to dress so that no mode of attire may be considered proper if it distracts from or is disruptive of the positive learning environment of the school."

  —Tangipahoa Parish School System, Louisiana

Shoes

Be sure your shoes are shined and in good repair. Don't wear shoes with run-down heels or a worn, "cracked" look. Be sure your shoes go with your dress or suit. And don't let your shoes "dress you down." By that we mean that the style of your shoes should be as dressy as the clothes you're wearing. A pair of sandals, for example, would destroy the classic look of a conservative business suit.

Jewelry

Go easy on the jewelry. For men, a ring and a wristwatch are plenty. Women should wear conservative gold, silver, or pearl earrings; avoid anything dangling or faddish. One ring on each hand is fine, plus a bracelet and a watch.

If you wear a ring or stud in your nose, lip, eyebrow, or tongue, our advice is to remove it for the interview.

Cleanliness

Your body should be squeaky-clean and odor-free, and your clothes should be clean as well. Don't wear anything to the interview that has a spot or stain (including sweat stains).

Before the interview, examine your clothes carefully in a strong light; if you have the slightest doubt about whether a spot will show, have the garment laundered or dry-cleaned. Also look for any tears or moth holes that should be mended.

This is all just common sense, of course, but it's amazing how many stories we've heard of candidates who wore crumpled, soiled clothing to interviews. One interviewer told us about a woman who came to the interview wearing a dress that had both armpits torn out—not a great first impression!

Men's fingernails should be trimmed and clean. Women should trim their nails to a conservative length, at least for the interview, and wear a neutral color of nail polish. Avoid bright reds, bright pinks, greens, blues, blacks, and nail art.

Hair

Men should have their hair cut or trimmed before the interview, including beards or mustaches. Facial hair is fine, but keep it groomed.

Women should wear their hair in a conservative style and make sure it's clean and shiny. If you have very long hair, it might be a good idea to tie it back or pull it up onto your head for the interview. Most image experts advise against wearing long hair down over a business suit.

Makeup

Women should use makeup conservatively for the interview. Avoid too much eyeliner, mascara, and blush, and wear lipstick in a pink, coral, or red— something that coordinates with your outfit. Stay away from blues, greens, blacks, and purples.

Body Language

In the course of our surveys, we had a very interesting interview with a behavioral specialist who sits on interview committees for a suburban school district in New Hampshire. Her insight is enormously valuable, because it applies her expertise as a behavioral specialist to the field of education. When asked what she learned from a teacher candidate's body language during interviews, she answered this way:

> *I look for body language that demonstrates self-confidence. I want strong eye contact, a firm handshake, and open posture. I look for movement that indicates uneasiness when new information is presented. I like it when I am able to read the applicant's reaction to information I present. Often, when job duties or responsibilities are presented, the candidate's mouth is saying "yes," but the body language clearly indicates that he or she is not receptive to the job. This helps in screening out some candidates.*
>
> *I also like to see how the body responds under pressure. The body language at the interview will give me insight as to what I can expect in the future. In addition, a friendly smile is always welcome. After all, they will be working with children, and we don't want the children to be frightened.*

> "The more nervous and 'fidgety' applicant will almost never get the job. Those who appear at ease, comfortable, and relaxed will always come out on top."
> —Director of bands and music curriculum and member of the interview committee for a rural school district in Texas

Eye Contact

We communicate with one another in many ways, but none is more important than eye contact. Eyes hold a world of emotions that are easily read.

> "Making eye contact is important. Also, how a person stands or walks can give hints to possible strengths or weaknesses."
> —Instructional coordinator and member of the interview committee for a suburban school district in Virginia

When you respond to a question during an interview, maintain eye contact with the members of the panel. Don't focus on only one of the interviewers, but look from one to another. Direct eye contact implies honesty and sincerity. If your eyes dart around the room as you speak, you take on a "shifty-eyed" look, which implies dishonesty. And whatever you do, don't stare at the ceiling, because that sends the message that you're bored.

Also maintain direct eye contact with each panel member who is speaking. This shows that you're interested and attentive to what the person is saying.

If you find it difficult to look someone in the eye, talk to the person's eyebrows—no one will ever know the difference.

Facial Expressions

Did you know that your facial expressions can cause physiological reactions in your body? This was proven in a study by a team of psychologists at Clark University in Worcester, Massachusetts. If your face is screwed up tight with a look of anxiety, you'll feel anxious. Likewise, if you concentrate on relaxing the muscles in your face, your body will react by relaxing all over. It's a cause-and-effect thing, with one feeding off the other.

Other facial expressions to avoid are frowns, "tight" lips, and squinted eyes; these all convey distrust or dislike of what is being said.

The bottom line is that you should work on keeping your facial expressions pleasant and relaxed, always ready for a smile when appropriate. A smile is a wonderful thing. An honest, sincere smile can convey enthusiasm, confidence, and control, even if you feel anything but enthusiastic, confident, or in control of the situation. It also goes a long way toward masking your nervousness and insecurities and puts the interviewer at ease. A smile says, "I like you," "I agree with you," and "I'm happy and comfortable to be here."

The Handshake

There are three kinds of handshakes: limp, firm, and vice-grip. Obviously, a firm handshake is what you want to work on.

A limp handshake evokes many subtexts, none of them good: disinterest, insecurity, weakness, and nervousness. And the old-fashioned Victorian handshake that extends only the fingers is the most distasteful of all because it says, "I don't really want to touch you because I don't trust you."

A bone-crushing handshake, on the other hand, evokes a subtext of aggression and wanting to take control.

A proper handshake is one in which you extend your entire hand, grasp the hand of the other person "skin-to-skin," give it one firm shake, and then let go. Be sure to return the same amount of pressure as you're given. Don't hang on too long, or you'll give the impression that you're "taking over."

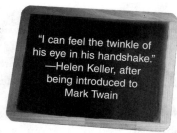

"I can feel the twinkle of his eye in his handshake."
—Helen Keller, after being introduced to Mark Twain

If shaking hands is awkward for you, now is the time to develop a firm, impressive grip. To do this, you need to practice. Your small networking group (see chapter 6) is a good place to start, because all of you are in the same predicament, and you can all use the practice. If you make it a habit to shake hands with one another every time you get together, you'll eventually feel comfortable with it. At that point you'll be ready to graduate to the next step, which is to look the person in the eye and call him or her by name as you shake hands.

Keep practicing until it becomes second nature.

Posture

As you walk into the interview room, stand straight with your head held high; this shows that you're confident and happy to be there. If you enter the room slowly, with a shuffle and a lowered head, you give the opposite impression.

> "I usually look for someone who seems relaxed in the shoulders. Constant shifting or crossing and uncrossing legs can be distracting. I wouldn't hold it against someone, but if my choice was between someone who fidgeted a lot and someone who at least appeared collected, it would be no contest."
> —8th-grade teacher and member of the hiring committee for a suburban district in Illinois

The ideal posture during an interview is to sit up, lean forward with arms uncrossed, make eye contact, and smile, if appropriate. This is known as an "affirmative posture." A "negative posture" is one in which you slouch in your chair, head down, arms crossed, making no eye contact.

If an interviewer leans back as you're speaking, do the same. This indicates that you might be coming on a little too strong. But be ready to lean forward again if you suddenly feel excited or passionate about something that's being said, or as soon as the interviewer leans forward and resumes an affirmative posture.

Hand Gestures

Hand gestures have a subtext all their own. Here are some common gestures you should avoid during a job interview:

- Stroking your chin
- Twisting your ear
- Scratching yourself—anywhere!
- Biting your nails
- Cracking your knuckles
- Pushing back your cuticles as you speak
- Jingling anything (keys, coins, and so on)

- Unwinding paper clips
- Fidgeting with or tapping a pen or pencil
- Playing with your rings, bracelet, earrings, or necklace
- Picking up anything and laying it back down
- Grooming yourself in any way (for example, smoothing your clothing or picking lint off your sleeve)
- Smoothing your hair back
- Rubbing your eye
- Tugging at your collar
- Straightening or smoothing the knot in your tie
- Placing one hand on the back of your neck
- Crossing and uncrossing your fingers
- Fingering your throat
- Leaning back and placing both hands behind your head
- Clasping and unclasping your fingers
- Holding your fingers in front of your mouth
- Wringing your hands

These gestures are distracting and annoying, and they send dozens of different negative messages: nervousness, doubt, distaste, or the indication that you might be lying. One way to control your hands, of course, is to keep them clasped throughout the interview. That isn't the best idea, but it is a solution in extreme cases. The best thing is to let your hands fall naturally on the chair's arms, or on the table if you're leaning forward, or (best of all) to hold a pen in one hand, poised over your notepad.

Head Gestures

Head gestures are telling as well. A nod sends a positive subtext: "Yes, I agree with what you're saying" or "I like you." A shake of the head, on the other hand, gives the impression that you don't like the person or that you don't like what is being said. Be careful that you don't nod constantly, however, or you'll send a senseless subtext.

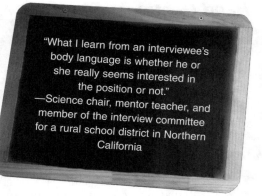

"What I learn from an interviewee's body language is whether he or she really seems interested in the position or not."
—Science chair, mentor teacher, and member of the interview committee for a rural school district in Northern California

Wait until you agree with something that's being said, and then nod. The nod is very effective if used with discretion.

Foot and Leg Gestures

Here are some feet and leg gestures to avoid during an interview:

- Shuffling your feet
- Moving your foot in and out of your shoe
- Tapping your foot
- Swinging a crossed leg
- Crossing and uncrossing your legs

If you're sitting at a table during the interview, feet and leg gestures aren't nearly as obvious as hand and head gestures. Be aware of them, however, and try to keep your feet and legs still.

Voice and Speech

You'll be doing a lot of talking during your interview, so it's important that you have a pleasant, well-modulated voice. When you're being interviewed for a job, there's a natural tendency for your pitch to get higher and higher, so make a concerted effort to lower your voice to a richly modulated tone. Then raise your voice occasionally to make a point, always returning to the lower pitch. Whatever you do, don't speak in a monotone.

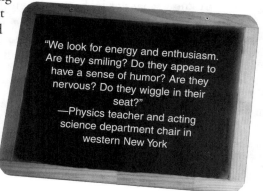

"We look for energy and enthusiasm. Are they smiling? Do they appear to have a sense of humor? Are they nervous? Do they wiggle in their seat?"
—Physics teacher and acting science department chair in western New York

Speed of Speech

Nervousness not only causes your pitch to rise, it causes "fast talk," too. The more nervous you are, the faster you'll talk. Rushing your words reveals insecurity with your answers, embarrassment, awkwardness, or that you just want to get the interview over with as soon as possible. Conversely, someone who speaks slowly conveys confidence, sincerity, and a feeling of being comfortable with the interview.

Patterns of Speech

Everyone has a certain cadence or pattern to their speech, punctuated with pauses, which are often effective, or with annoying fillers, which are not. Common fillers include phrases like "You know," "Uhhh," "I mean," and clearing of the throat. Chances are you use fillers when you speak and don't even realize it. The only way you'll know for sure is to listen to yourself on an audiotape or video-tape; you'll probably be surprised at all the fillers. Try to eliminate them as much as possible before you start interviewing. Ask your family, friends, and the members of your networking group to point them out if they sneak in without your realizing it.

> "An interviewee's body language tells me how comfortable he is, what really excites him, if he is unsure of himself. A person who knows what's he's talking about and is excited about it leans forward, smiles more, and makes eye contact."
> —Member of an interview committee for an inner-city school district in Detroit

Use the information in this chapter to sharpen your personal appeal. Of course, you won't know what needs sharpening until you see yourself as others see you, and this is where your networking group comes in. Use the videotaped mock interviews (see chapter 6) to scrutinize your dress, grooming, body language, and voice patterns. When you're aware of your flaws, it isn't difficult to correct them.

CHAPTER 8

Your Conduct During the Interview

We could compare the job search to running a 1,500-meter race—four laps around the track. By the end of the first lap, you've located the job openings. By the end of lap two, you've completed the paperwork. If you survive the third lap of the race, you've made the paper cut, and you're ready for that final gut-wrenching lap: the interview itself.

If you're one of eight contestants in the race, your chances of winning the gold medal depend on one final thing—how you conduct yourself during the interview.

A Positive Attitude Is the Key

Walk through any bookstore, and you'll see dozens of books on the impact of a positive attitude, including the ever-popular *The Power of Positive Thinking* by Norman Vincent Peale. Countless motivational speakers have touted the virtues of a positive attitude for decades. There's a reason for this: Your attitude is the key to your success.

Jack Nicklaus in his book *Golf My Way* (Simon and Schuster, 1998) even tells us that positive imaging can improve your golf game. For example, if you picture your ball lying 250 yards off the tee, right in the center of the fairway, it's much more likely to happen than if you scold yourself with negative talk such as "Don't lift your head" or "Don't top the ball." This kind of talk, in fact, produces exactly the result you don't want, because it's the last thought you have before hitting the golf ball.

"Tell yourself that you are the best applicant, and then go with confidence to the interview, feeling prepared to be their next new hire!"
—Science chair, mentor teacher, and member of the interview committee for a rural district in Northern California

So, the key is to have a positive attitude, always expecting the best to happen. But how can this help you during your job interview? Well, what works in golf also works in life. If you picture yourself doing well and being chosen to fill the position, it's more likely to happen.

Most candidates enter the interview room feeling like they're on trial—as if the interview panel will sit in judgment of how they perform. If there's a table between the candidate and the panel—and there usually is—it creates an even greater barrier. However, the truth of the matter is this:

You are not on trial!

- The table that sits between you is only a *perceived* barrier.
- The panel wants to *help* you.
- They *want* you to sell yourself.
- They *want* you to be the one they hire.

You see, they're on your side; it's not an adversarial situation. They want to find a terrific teacher to fill the vacancy, and they *hope* you're the one.

As you sit in the lobby waiting for your turn to be interviewed, remember that you must make a great first impression—there are no second chances. Think of how you feel sitting in an audience when an enter-tainer or comedian steps on stage; it takes only 10 seconds to know whether you like the person.

It's the same way with a job interview. You have to make them like you in the first 10 seconds—no retakes, no do-overs. So visualize yourself doing just that. Then, as your name is called and you walk into the interview room, stand straight, hold your head high, shake hands, and smile as you look each panel member in the eye.

> "Speak from your heart… your love for children will come through."
> —High school special education teacher in Wisconsin

Questions You Should Ask

At some point during the interview, you'll be expected to ask questions of your own. Often, interviewees take a somewhat defensive role, merely listening and responding to the questions asked by the panel. Depending on how comfortable you are, you might not feel like breaking in with a question of your own. Then again, depending on how things are going, you might feel at ease asking a ques-tion at any point.

In either case, you definitely want to prepare questions beforehand. If your questions are not answered in the course of the interview, be sure to ask them before you conclude. Typically, toward the end of the interview, the panel will ask whether you have any questions. At this point an answer such as "No, I think you've answered them all" or "I can't think of anything" doesn't look good. They expect you to be curious about things, and if you've thought this out in advance, it will impress them.

Don't rely on memory for these important questions. Practice asking them out loud before the day of the interview, and then jot them down on a 3 × 5 card and bring the card with you to the interview. The interview panel will be impressed that you put some forethought into the interview process.

> "Don't be afraid to ask questions. Prepare some, even on a card, so that you appear to be well-prepared."
> —8th-grade teacher and member of the hiring committee for a suburban district in Illinois

Before we get into examples of questions you might want to ask, we want to caution you about being too aggressive with your questioning. Keep in mind that you are the interviewee. Yes, it's true: You are interviewing them, too. You want to find out whether the job is a good fit. And using your mission statement as a guide (see chapter 1), there are certain things you must learn about the position, the school, the district, and so on. But remember to ask your questions in such a way that you don't seem to be "taking over" the interview.

> "Jot down any questions that come to mind during the interview."
> —8th-grade teacher and member of the hiring committee for a suburban district in Illinois

Also, we recommend avoiding certain kinds of questions; we'll talk about these a little later.

Ask Questions That Showcase Your Talents

Back to the questions you'll want to ask: There's a little twist that can work for you just as well as it works for the interview panel. We mentioned in chapter 6 that interviewers' questions often have underlying purposes. For example, when they ask, "What are your strengths and weaknesses?" or "Tell us about yourself," what they really want to know is, "Why should we hire you?" Well, there's no reason your questions can't have an underlying purpose as well—to showcase your talents. Here are a few examples of questions you might ask:

- I've had some experience working on a school yearbook, and I really enjoyed working with the students. Do you have a yearbook?

- I've always considered myself a team player, and I feel it's important and more productive when staff members can put their heads together. Do the teachers at this school plan or work on projects together?

- I have experience in choral music and theater production, and I would like to be involved in that in some way. Does your school offer any music or drama for the kids or the community?

The underlying purpose of these questions is to show that you have talents that can be of benefit to the school and the community. They also demonstrate that you are an enthusiastic team player, willing to give more time and energy than any of the other candidates the panel is interviewing.

You can ask other questions that might impress the panel. These will demonstrate your knowledge, enthusiasm, and interest. When we asked interview panel members what questions they felt teacher candidates should ask during an interview, we got these suggestions:

1. In what ways do the parents get involved with the school?
2. What kinds of cross-cultural activities do you offer to the kids and the community (assuming that ethnic diversity exists)?
3. What new innovations or programs has the school or district implemented (for your grade level or subject area)?
4. Does the school or district have a general discipline plan (such as Canter & Canter or *Assertive Discipline*)?
5. Does the school or district have a mentor-teacher program?
6. Are the classrooms self-contained or departmentalized?
7. Is there team teaching?
8. Do you offer professional growth opportunities for new teachers?
9. What are the strengths of this school/district?
10. How do administrators offer teacher support if the need arises?
11. How would you characterize school morale?
12. When will you notify candidates of your hiring decision?

This is not an exhaustive list; it's meant to suggest some ideas for you to consider. Some might not seem important or applicable to you, but because they were suggested by members of hiring panels, we think they should be given some weight.

Direct Your Questions Appropriately

One great piece of advice came from a school principal we interviewed, who said that the teacher candidate should *never* address a specific member of the panel. For example, you should never ask, "Ms. Johnson, what is your district's policy regarding bilingual education?"

This is a mistake for several reasons. First, Ms. Johnson might not know about the policy, or there might not be a specific policy. Also, Ms. Johnson might not agree with the district's philosophy of bilingual education, which could result in a very awkward moment for everyone. The results of this kind of questioning leave Ms. Johnson looking bad and feeling embarrassed, which means you score badly.

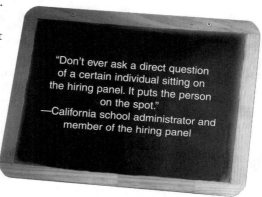

"Don't ever ask a direct question of a certain individual sitting on the hiring panel. It puts the person on the spot."
—California school administrator and member of the hiring panel

If you think a question is legitimate, you should ask it, of course, but direct it to the entire committee. One word of advice: Always ask sincere questions that are *important to you*. If your questions impress the interview committee or give you a chance to tell them something more about yourself, that's simply an added bonus.

The important thing to remember is this: You should come prepared with a few well-thought-out questions; that will impress the interview panel.

Questions to Avoid

Just as important as the questions you ask are those you don't. There are some questions you should simply avoid asking. Most of these are fairly obvious. But, according to our hiring panel contacts throughout the United States, a few words should be mentioned here about indiscreet, inappropriate questions. Then there are questions that are not necessarily indiscreet or inappropriate, but that, in a subtle way, can put you on thin ice and work against you.

Before we list the questions to avoid, however, let us mention one caveat that applies to your whole demeanor, including your questions of the hiring panel: the matter of *attitude*. If your attitude is perceived as even slightly questionable, it probably will undo all the positives you've worked so hard to develop and communicate. We don't want you to mess up a good thing because of a slip of the tongue or an indiscretion. So avoid any question that makes your attitude suspect. If there's something you think you really must ask, and you're unsure how it will be taken, use your own judgment, but conventional wisdom would say "forget it." Or reword it so that the attitude factor is taken out of the mix. You get the point.

Sometimes it's not so much the question itself, but something in the inflection or tone of your voice or in your body language that might tip your hand in the minds of the panel and work against you. You get only one shot at this stuff, so choose your words *and your tone* carefully.

With that sermonette preached, let's move on to a list of questions or topics we think you should avoid. Most of them have come from principals, mentor teachers, curriculum personnel, and others who sit on hiring panels in their districts.

The most obvious topics to avoid are at the top of the list:

1. **Anything related to salary.**
2. **Benefits:** School office personnel, your teacher association representative, or a teacher handbook can fill you in on this subject.
3. **School hours:** This information can be obtained from the school secretary or other teachers. Most schools have a standard school day: start at 8:30 or 9 a.m.; dismiss at 3 or 3:30 p.m.
4. **Taking time off for personal business:** Don't ask the members of the panel; get a copy of the school's teacher handbook.
5. **Anything remotely sexist.**
6. **A breakdown of the community's ethnicity:** An exception is, of course, if you're a bilingual teacher and this information is necessary.
7. **Any questions that pertain to the community's religious, political, or socioeconomic breakdown:** You get into touchy areas here, and the chances are too great that your questions will be misread. This information is available through other sources.
8. **Any question that could be interpreted to mean that you're not totally committed to the teaching profession:** For example, "Do you expect your teachers to take work home often?"
9. **Extracurricular responsibilities:** Don't ask anything that might cause the panel to question your work ethic or attitude.
10. **Overstressing concerns regarding discipline:** Don't ask question after question about discipline-related issues.

11. **Questions regarding the "bargaining unit":** You're talking to the wrong folks if you bring up unions or teachers' associations here.

12. **The prospects of transferring to another grade level or department:** Wait until you're hired, and then pursue this concern at the appropriate time.

38 Ways to Turn Off an Interview Committee

We asked every interviewer who took part in our survey 20 or so questions, including "What is the biggest turnoff during an interview?" Some of the answers were what we expected, but others were quite surprising. Here are the answers we got.

1. Your Cell Phone

Turn off your cell phone before the interview. Better yet, leave it in your car during the interview.

2. Tardiness

To land a job, you need every advantage—and the last time we checked, tardiness wasn't one of them. First impressions are lasting impressions; being late makes a bad first impression.

We suggest that you arrive early enough to visit the restroom and check your appearance. (You never know—you might have a piece of spinach stuck on your tooth, smudged eye shadow, or something unbuttoned.) Remember, tardiness is a form of rudeness. Don't be rude.

3. Inappropriate Clothing/Dress

Women will never go wrong wearing a nice dress or suit. Men should wear slacks and a sport jacket or a business suit (depending on the school district), always with a tie. We were shocked at the number of times "unshined shoes" cropped up. Don't just dust them off—*shine them!* (See the section "Dress and Grooming" in chapter 7 for more tips.)

4. Dangling Earrings or Long, Brightly Painted Fingernails

We've found that many interviewers aren't crazy about either of these. In one case, a teacher with long, painted nails was being interviewed for a kindergarten position. None of the panel members could picture her working with 5- or 6-year-olds, so they hired someone else. As far as earrings go, you might opt for a pair of conservative gold or silver studs instead.

5. Body Piercing

If you normally wear a ring or stud in your tongue, lip, nose, or eyebrow, you might want to remove it before your interview. Although this is a fashionable trend and you're certainly entitled to pierce your body if you want to, you should be aware that, at least in our survey, body piercing is often a major turnoff for interviewers.

6. Poor Personal Hygiene

If that smell wasn't there before you arrived, and if it disappears when you leave, you're in big trouble. Poor personal hygiene is inexcusable. Most people are offended by it. We can't imagine a candidate coming to an interview with bad breath or body odor, yet it happens. Don't be one of these losers. You'll never get that job—count on it.

7. Chewing Gum or Smoking During the Interview

While this is hard to believe, interviewers tell us it does happen. Gum chewing might be an oversight; ditch your gum before you leave home. Here are two thoughts about smoking:

- If you can't make it through an interview without a smoke, how will you teach for hours at a time?
- If teachers are role models, what example are you setting for students when you smoke?

8. Poor Social Skills

Review the "don'ts" from chapter 7, including poor eye contact, "dressing down," and covering your mouth as you speak. Work on a firm, steady hand-shake.

9. Giving Pat, Canned, or Insincere Answers

Interview committees can read these like a book. We suggest that you practice pausing at least a second or two before responding to any question. This gives the impression that you are thoughtful, relaxed, and poised. Practice responding to the sample questions listed in chapter 6 until your answers sound as natural and unrehearsed as possible. Finally, be honest.

10. Telling the Committee What You Think They Want to Hear

If you're so desperate for a job that your answers reflect only what you think they want to hear, rather than what you really feel, you might end up with a job you're unhappy with, and the district ends up with an employee it wishes it hadn't hired.

11. An Attitude That Is Too Relaxed and Informal

It's good to be relaxed, but familiarity can be overdone and work against you. You don't want to appear disinterested in the questions or disrespectful of the panel members.

12. Poor Communication of Ideas

One cause of this is a lack of practice at responding to possible panel questions. Even if you have thought out a response in advance, you still might be unable to articulate it clearly. Again, we suggest practice, practice, practice.

13. Not Sticking to the Subject

When answering questions, be concise; resist the temptation to impress the panel with your wealth of college knowledge. Stick to the subject, and don't say anything that doesn't improve upon the silence.

14. Not Knowing When to Close or Stop Talking

Often, the more you ramble, the more you paint yourself into a corner. By rambling, you reveal one of the following:

- You don't really know the answer, but with enough tries, you hope to stumble on it.
- You're unable to express yourself succinctly.

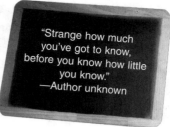

"Strange how much you've got to know, before you know how little you know."
—Author unknown

Hiring committees are seldom interested in soliloquies. They appreciate a brief, concise, well-articulated response.

15. Answers That Are Too Defensive or Aggressive

Either of these creates an awkward, uncomfortable interview. Interviews are not meant to be confrontational. Don't come to the interview with an "attitude."

16. Negativity

Interview panels *do not* enjoy interviewing negative candidates, and negative candidates almost *never* get the jobs. Schools are looking for positive, upbeat teachers. Avoid negativity.

17. Badmouthing

Don't criticize or badmouth another school, district, or person, including a previous employer. This has never helped anyone get a job—in *any* profession. Everything you say might be true, but it doesn't help your cause. The committee will simply assume you'll badmouth their school if they hire you.

18. Being a Know-It-All

Don't go by the old expression "If you've got it, flaunt it!" Your responses will reveal your command of the subject matter. Trying to unduly impress the interview committee with your boundless knowledge, giving the impression that you're an expert on all educational topics, will just turn them off. "Selling yourself" has its limits—don't carry on ad nauseam. The committee can tell the difference between a phony and the real thing. A little knowledge can be dangerous, so play it safe.

19. Indications That You Think Your Methods and Philosophies Are the Only Ones

This is closely related to being a know-it-all, so the same advice applies: Watch it, or you'll appear arrogant. Don't insult the panel: They've been around much longer than you. You must have opinions about and some understanding of teaching methods, but remember, you're just getting started in this profession.

20. Inflexibility

Because teachers work in an environment with so many variables, they must be flexible. Schedules change, interruptions happen, equipment fails, employees don't show, children get sick—the list is endless. If you appear to be a team player who isn't easily flustered, you'll have a much better chance of being hired.

21. Haughty, Arrogant, or Superior Manner

To mask insecurity, some people *act* haughty, arrogant, or superior; others *are* haughty, arrogant, and think they're superior. Whichever the case, such behavior counts as a strike against you. You need to be a bit humble in this situation, even though you are trying to sell yourself. Remember: You don't have a job— they do.

22. Bragging; Going Beyond Reasonable Selling of Yourself; Flaunting Yourself

Again, if you're good, you don't have to prove it through arrogance or a haughty manner. Rest assured that the interview committee knows the difference between confidence and an overbearing, obnoxious "sales job."

23. Lack of Membership in Professional Organizations

Memberships in professional organizations are very impressive. They show you have interest, enthusiasm, and professionalism. Most professional organizations are there to help you; get acquainted with them. (We've included a list of such organizations in the appendix.) Be prepared to drop a few names, if possible. This is definitely an opportunity to give yourself a leg up; take advantage of it.

"Have opinions about current educational issues, because they *will* come up in the interview."
—K–12 P.E. teacher in Charlottesville, Virginia

24. Not Knowing Current Educational Trends, Methods, and Issues

Being new to the profession, you won't be expected to know *all* the new and current things going on, but you should definitely know the "hottest" ones. Be prepared to mention the latest educational buzzwords on occasion. A "clueless look" in response to a question will be a red flag to the committee.

25. Candidates Who Think They Have Finished Learning Because They're Out of School

This kind of attitude displays inflexibility. Learning should be a lifelong mission for everyone—especially those in the teaching profession. This attitude also calls your work ethic into question.

26. No Knowledge of the School or Community

Do your homework: Know something about the basic demographics of the school and the community (see chapter 6).

27. Displaying Stupidity

Never ask questions about salary and benefits. And avoid asking questions that reveal you know nothing about the school district or the community. If you're asked a question and you know absolutely nothing about the subject, don't wing it; it's better to say you don't know the answer than to insult the committee by blowing smoke.

28. Poor Grammar

Is your grammar adequate? If your best friend won't tell you, ask someone else—someone who'll be completely honest. If colloquial family or regional grammar problems crop up in your speech, you need to be aware of and correct them. Poor grammar can be a *real* handicap.

29. Lack of Self-Confidence

It's natural to feel apprehensive and a little short on confidence in a stressful, unfamiliar setting, and interviews certainly fall into that category. To overcome this, we suggest you come to the interview as prepared as possible. Spend time rehearsing your responses to questions you might be asked, and practice role-playing a few mock interviews (see chapter 6). These exercises will help you feel more confident during the interview.

If your self-confidence is still a little shaky when you arrive for the interview, you can usually give the *impression* of confidence by replacing your anxious frown with a sincere smile.

30. Lackluster Performance

If a member of the committee checks your vital signs at any time during the interview, assume you're not doing well. Be upbeat and positive. A little nervousness is normal, but put that adrenaline to good use. Schools need intelligent, dynamic teachers. Present that image.

31. Negative Body Language

As we discussed in chapter 7, negative body language can include everything from a closed-up or defensive posture to poor eye contact, slouching, or a scowl. Sit in a relaxed, comfortable fashion. Make eye contact with the person asking the question, and then make eye contact with the rest of the members of the panel as you answer the question. Be pleasant and sincere.

32. Being Unprepared

In addition to being prepared to answer the panel's questions, bring your portfolio to the interview, along with 3 × 5 cards that have questions to ask at the end of the interview. Also bring a pen and notepaper, preferably affixed inside a manila folder. And plan to arrive at least 10 minutes early for your interview.

33. No Questions for the Interview Panel

If you're *really* interested in working at a particular school, you should have some specific, intelligent questions to ask about that school. Your questions will show the panel that you're interested in knowing more and will give them a chance to brag a little—definitely good PR.

34. Playing Politics

Members of an interview committee act collectively. Even if you know a member of the committee—or you know someone who knows someone who knows someone on the committee—you must not skirt the process by trying to influence an individual panel member. This puts that person in an awkward position and might well backfire. Go through the process like everyone else, and avoid the temptation to make political contacts to better your cause.

35. "Not My Job" Syndrome

You're interviewing for a position that has certain expectations. If you make it a point to tell the committee which duties you would rather not perform, they'll be relieved—because they can hire someone else. Hiring panels are looking for workers, not shirkers.

36. Blaming Students for Their Failure to Do Well

It's hard to imagine that teachers would blame students for their lack of success when one of their jobs is to motivate them. The school and teacher can and do make a difference. Don't be an "elitist-defeatist."

37. More Interest in the Compensation Package Than the Kids

Unless the interview committee brings it up, *never* ask about salary or benefits. This information is public knowledge and is readily available by other means.

38. Lack of Passion for Kids and Teaching

Teaching is not just a job—it's a way of life. When you talk to the interview committee, they should see someone who's excited about the profession. Your body language should show it; your words should tell it; your eyes should flash it. Good teachers are usually good performers. Show some passion!

At the End of the Interview

In this chapter we've given you lots of "dos" and "don'ts." Be aware of the latter, but don't dwell on them. Emphasize instead the "dos," and remember: You're a strong candidate, or you wouldn't have made it this far.

If you run this final lap in style—if your attitude is great, your questions appropriate, and your responses impressive and tactful—you're sure to win the race.

Finally, at the conclusion of your interview, stand, smile, thank the panel for the opportunity to interview, and walk confidently from the room with visions of the gold medal that will surely be yours when the race results are announced.

You might think you're done now, but you're not. You still need to follow up after the interview to help clinch the job. See chapter 9 for hints on doing this effectively.

Following Up After the Interview

The job search process doesn't end with the interview. You can still influence the hiring panel in two important ways—by sending a thank-you letter and by placing a follow-up phone call. This chapter gives you tips on doing both effectively and also offers some words of encouragement in case you didn't get the job.

The Thank-You Letter

Be sure to follow up after the interview with a thank-you letter to the person who interviewed you or to the entire hiring panel, addressing the letter in care of the panel's chairperson. Not only is this proper etiquette, it's also a very smart thing to do. It's a way of gently reminding the interviewer of who you are and distinguishing yourself from the dozen or so applicants who might have been interviewed for the position. You should take this opportunity to sell yourself one more time. You might be the only applicant who makes this effort, so this will create a positive impression, especially if you're already near the top of the list.

Write the letter as soon as possible, preferably the same day you're interviewed. You want your letter to arrive *before* the decision is made. After all, proper etiquette isn't the *only* reason you're sending it; you hope it will sway the panel.

This is the structure of a good thank-you letter:

- **Paragraph 1:** Thank the interviewer for considering you for the position. Mention something specific you especially appreciated about the meeting.
- **Paragraph 2:** Tactfully review your qualifications and how you feel they are a match for the position.
- **Paragraph 3:** Thank the interviewer for his or her time, and express your continued interest in the position.

Figure 9.1 is an example of a well-written thank-you letter.

Carson MacAllister
8506 Turner Avenue
Indianapolis, IN 46226

February 27, 2007

Dr. Martin Stuart
Superintendent
Hammond Unified School District
932 Palerma Avenue
Hammond, IN 47301

Dear Dr. Stuart:

Thank you for meeting with me today to discuss the position you have available for a seventh-grade language arts teacher.

It was encouraging to hear of your recent purchase of new computers and writing-skills software. As we discussed during our conversation, I have had a great deal of experience using this software in the past, and it would be exciting for me to be involved in your new program. It will be rewarding to see how quickly your students' writing skills will improve.

Again, many thanks for your time and attention. I am very interested in your school district and would enjoy working at Montbello School as your new language arts teacher. I look forward to hearing from you in the near future.

Sincerely,

Carson MacAllister

Figure 9.1: An example of a thank-you letter.

Follow-Up Phone Calls

It's also a smart idea to follow up your interview and thank-you letter with a telephone call. In fact, certain situations demand it:

- If you have additional or recent information that might sway the decision in your favor.

- You wrote a thank-you letter but haven't heard anything for two weeks.

- You have received another job offer, and you need to know where you stand before making the decision.

- You feel the interview went badly, and you want to request a second interview.

A survey from CareerBuilder.com found that 15 percent of hiring managers would not hire someone who did not send a thank-you note after the interview. About 32 percent said they'd consider the candidate but would think less of that person.

Before you place the call, brace yourself for the possibility that they have hired someone else without notifying you. If this happens, you should try to find out why they hired someone else. Ask what you can do to improve your interview skills in the future.

Some administrators will give you helpful advice—if you ask. But don't expect them to tell you why you weren't hired. Lawsuits have been initiated over such information, and administrators are told not to discuss personnel decisions.

Now, if you're mentally prepared to make that call, here are some ideas of what you might say:

> *Dr. Stuart? This is Carson MacAllister. We met on February 27th, when I was interviewed for the seventh-grade language arts position at Montbello School. I wanted to know whether you've reached your decision...*

If the decision has not been made, you might want to add something like this to your conversation:

> *I have some ideas on how we might expand the Edgar Writing Skills program to help the eighth graders as well. I would like to meet with you again to talk about this possibility...*

or

> *Is there anything further you would like to know about me that might help you with your decision?*

or

> *Do you know when you will make your decision? I have another job offer pending, and I would like to know whether I am still being considered for the position at your school.*

If you have no doubt that your interview went badly, you might be upfront with the interviewer and ask if you can meet again:

> *Dr. Stuart, I don't feel the interview afforded you the opportunity to see my full potential. Would it be possible for me to stop by to talk to you once more before you make your decision?*

By the way, if the position is filled, don't give up. Keep calling back once a month or so. Every situation is different, so be sensitive to the reaction you receive when you continue to call back so that you don't become a nuisance. Remind the interviewer who you are and that you're still interested in other positions that open up in the future. You might have been a very close second. You never know. Vacancies occur at odd times throughout the year, and you might just be the one who gets the job because of your persistence.

> Of the teacher candidates and newly hired teachers in our survey, 37 percent said they followed up their interviews with a thank-you letter and/or a telephone call.

Be Patient and Positive

If you haven't been offered a position even after several interviews that seemed to go well, try not to get discouraged. Research shows that people often receive many rejections before finally being hired. If you've had a number of rejections so far, keep looking ahead. Your next interview may well result in a "yes."

Don't let the rejections get you down; there are many reasons that someone else might have been hired that have nothing to do with you personally. There might have been three or four candidates who were equally qualified for the position, but one might have had something as simple as an additional credential that would give the school district more options in the future. And if you interviewed for a position as a high school history/geography teacher, maybe they hired the one candidate who has been on three European tours as opposed to your one. That's

> "Don't lose hope. I was told by every interviewer that I was an exceptional candidate, then told that I was their second choice. If you really want to teach, if you can't picture yourself doing anything else, then you will eventually teach. I look back and am thankful I was able to resist the temptation to give up."
> —High school social studies teacher in New Jersey

not a reflection on you; it merely reflects your bad luck in competing against someone so well-traveled.

So don't beat yourself up and fill your mind with defeatist thoughts. If you do, those thoughts will grow and multiply, feeding on each other until your mind is so full of them that hope doesn't have a chance. If you're to keep your hopes alive, keep your mind clear of anything negative.

Don't let your dream of becoming a teacher die. You have a chance to be a life-changing influence in young lives. You've worked too hard for this, and it's too worthy a profession to abandon at this early stage. All it takes is a little patience, a little prayer, and a little time. It will come—and soon. We wish you much success!

Epilogue

Now you know the "inside secrets" of finding a teaching position, and you're sure to be the one who stands out from the rest, landing not just one but several job offers! Our hearts go with you in your pursuit. You'll love being a teacher: It's a rewarding, life-changing profession, the noblest of them all.

Perhaps Lee Iacocca said it best:

> *In a completely rational society, the best of us would aspire to be teachers and the rest of us would have to settle for something less, because passing civilization along from one generation to the next ought to be the highest honor and the highest responsibility anyone could have.*

Hang in there—it's worth it!

Jack Warner and Clyde Bryan

Educational Resources: Associations, State-Specific Contacts, and Overseas Opportunities

In this appendix you'll find contact information and Web sites for educational associations, state departments of education, state offices of teacher certification, and state affiliates of the National Education Association (NEA). You'll also find information about places to look for teaching opportunities outside the United States.

Educational Associations

These educational associations provide up-to-date news, conference information, publications, resources, and general support for teachers in various specific fields.

American Alliance for Health, Physical Education, Recreation, and Dance
1900 Association Dr.
Reston, VA 20191
800-213-7193
www.aahperd.org

American Association for Gifted Children at Duke University
Box 90270
Durham, NC 27708-0270
919-783-6152
www.aagc.org

American Association of Physics Teachers
One Physics Ellipse
College Park, MD 20740-3845
301-209-3311
www.aapt.org

American Counseling Association
5999 Stevenson Ave.
Alexandria, VA 22304-3300
800-347-6647
www.counseling.org

American Federation of Teachers, AFL-CIO
555 New Jersey Ave. NW
Washington, DC 20001
202-879-4400
www.aft.org

American Library Association
50 E. Huron
Chicago, IL 60611
800-545-2433
www.ala.org

American Mathematical Society
201 Charles St.
Providence, RI 02940-2294
800-321-4267
401-455-4000
www.ams.org

American Montessori Society
281 Park Ave. S.
New York, NY 10010
212-358-1256
www.americanmontessorisociety.org

American Speech-Language-Hearing Association
10801 Rockville Pike
Rockville, MD 20852
800-638-8255
www.asha.org

Association for Childhood Education International
17904 Georgia Ave., Ste. 215
Olney, MD 20832
800-423-3563
301-570-2111
www.acei.org

Association of Teacher Educators
1900 Association Dr., Ste. ATE
Reston, VA 20191
703-620-3110
www.ate1.org

Council for Advancement and Support of Education
1307 New York Ave. NW, Ste. 1000
Washington, DC 20005-4701
202-328-2273
www.case.org

Council for Children with Behavioral Disorders
1110 N. Glebe Rd., Ste. 300
Arlington, VA 22201-5704
888-232-7733
www.ccbd.net

Council for Elementary Science International
212 Townsend Hall
Columbia, MO 65211
314-882-4831
www.cesiscience.org

Council for Exceptional Children
1110 N. Glebe Rd., Ste. 300
Arlington, VA 22201-5704
888-232-7733
703-620-3660
www.cec.sped.org

MENC: The National Association for Music Education
1806 Robert Fulton Dr.
Reston, VA 20191
800-336-3768
703-860-4000
www.menc.org

Music Teachers National Association
441 Vine St., Ste. 505
Cincinnati, OH 45202
888-512-5278
513-421-1420
www.mtna.org

National Art Education Association
1916 Association Dr.
Reston, VA 20191-1590
703-860-8000
www.naea-reston.org

National Association for Bilingual Education
1030 15th St. NW
Washington, DC 20005
202-898-1829
www.nabe.org

National Association for Business Teacher Education
1914 Association Dr.
Reston, VA 22091
703-860-8300
www.educ.uidaho.edu/standards/national.htm

National Association for the Education of Young Children
1509 16th St. NW
Washington, DC 20036
800-424-2460
202-232-8777
www.naeyc.org

National Association of Biology Teachers
12030 Sunrise Valley Dr., Ste. 110
Reston, VA 20191
800-406-0775
703-264-9696
www.nabt.org

National Association of Industrial and Technical Teacher Educators
PO Box 1442
Portage, MI 49081-1442
613-387-3007
www.coe.uga.edu/naitte/

National Business Education Association
1914 Association Drive
Reston, VA 20191-1596
703-860-8300
www.nbea.org

National Career Development Association
305 N. Beech Circle
Broken Arrow, OK 74012
866-367-6232
918-663-7060
www.ncda.org

National Communication Association
1765 N St. NW
Washington, DC 20036
202-464-4622
www.natcom.org

National Council for the Social Studies
8555 16th St.
Silver Spring, MD 20910
301-588-1800
www.socialstudies.org

National Council of Teachers of English
1111 W. Kenyon Rd.
Urbana, IL 61801-1096
877-369-6283
217-328-3870
www.ncte.org

National Council of Teachers of Mathematics
1906 Association Dr.
Reston, VA 20191-1502
703-620-9840
www.nctm.org

National Education Association
1201 16th St. NW
Washington, DC 20036-3290
202-833-4000
www.nea.org

National Science Teachers Association
1840 Wilson Blvd.
Arlington, VA 22201-3000
703-243-7100
www.nsta.org

School Science and Mathematics Association
16734 Hamilton Ct.
Strongsville, OH 44149-5701
440-238-2633
www.ssma.org

State Departments of Education

State departments of education provide a wide range of information, including news, trends, recent press releases and legislation, and helpful resources. Their Web sites also offer links to job opportunities and, in most cases, the state's school report cards.

Alabama
Alabama Department of Education
50 North Ripley Street
PO Box 302101
Montgomery, AL 36104
www.alsde.edu/html/home.asp

Alaska
Alaska State Department of Education
801 W. 10th St., Ste. 200
Juneau, AK 99801-1878
907-465-2800
www.eed.state.ak.us
Job link: http://216.219.216.151

Arizona
Arizona Department of Education
1535 W. Jefferson St.
Phoenix, AZ 85007
800-352-4558
602-542-5393
www.ade.state.az.us
Job link: www.ade.state.az.us/empl_opp.asp

Arkansas
Arkansas Department of Education
4 Capitol Mall
Little Rock, AR 72201
501-682-4475
http://arkedu.state.ar.us
Job link: http://arkedu.state.ar.us/employment/employment.html

California

California Department of Education
1430 N Street
Sacramento, CA 95814
916-319-0800
www.cde.ca.gov
Job link: www.cde.ca.gov/re/di/jb/

Colorado

Colorado Department of Education
State Office Building
201 E. Colfax Ave.
Denver, CO 80203-1799
303-866-6600
www.cde.state.co.us/index_home.htm
Job link: www.cde.state.co.us/
cdemgmt/HR/jobs.htm

Connecticut

Connecticut State Department of
Education
165 Capitol Ave.
Hartford, CT 06145
860-713-6548
www.state.ct.us/sde/
Job link: www.state.ct.us/sde/employ/
jobs-main.htm

Delaware

Delaware Department of Education
John G. Townsend Building
401 Federal St., Ste. 2
Dover, DE 19901
302-739-4601
www.doe.k12.de.us
Job link: www.teachdelaware.com

District of Columbia

District of Columbia Public Schools
825 N. Capitol St. NE
Washington, DC 20002
202-724-4222
www.k12.dc.us/dcps/home.html
Job link: www.k12.dc.us/dcps/
opportunities/dcpshrhome.html

Florida

Florida Department of Education
Officer of the Commissioner
Turlington Building, Ste. 1514
325 W. Gaines St.
Tallahassee, FL 32399
850-245-0505
www.firn.edu/doe/
Job link: www.fldoe.org/
employment.asp

Georgia

Georgia Department of Education
1452 Twin Towers E.
Atlanta, GA 30334
404-657-9000
www.doe.k12.ga.us/index.asp
Job link: www.teachgeorgia.org/
job_search.aspx

Hawaii

Hawaii Department of Education
PO Box 2360
Honolulu, HI 96804
808-586-3230
http://doe.k12.hi.us
Job link: http://doe.k12.hi.us/
personnel/jobopportunities.htm

Idaho

Idaho State Department of Education
650 W. State St.
PO Box 83720
Boise, ID 83720-0027
800-432-4601
208-332-6800
www.sde.state.id.us/Dept/
Job link:
www.idahoeducationjobs.com/

Illinois

Illinois State Board of Education
100 N. 1st St.
Springfield, IL 62777
866-262-6663
www.isbe.state.il.us
Job link: www.isbe.net/
employment.htm

Indiana

Indiana Department of Education
Room 229
State House
Indianapolis, IN 46204-2798
317-232-0808
http://ideanet.doe.state.in.us
Job link: http://ideanet.doe.state.in.us/
peer/welcome.html

Iowa

Iowa Department of Education
Grimes State Office Building
Des Moines, IA 50319-0146
515-281-5294
www.state.ia.us/educate/
Job link: www.state.ia.us/educate/jobs/
index.html

Kansas

Kansas State Department of Education
120 SE 10th Ave.
Topeka, KS 66612
785-296-3204
www.ksbe.state.ks.us/Welcome.html
Job link:
www.kansasteachingjobs.com/

Kentucky

Kentucky Department of Education
500 Mero St., 19th Floor
Frankfort, KY 40601
502-564-3421
www.kde.state.ky.us
Job link: www.education.ky.gov/KDE/
HomePageRepository/jobs/default.htm

Louisiana

Louisiana Department of Education
PO Box 44064
Baton Rouge, LA 70804-9064
877-453-2721
www.doe.state.la.us/lde/index.html
Job link: www.teachlouisiana.net/
job.asp?PageID=3

Maine

Maine Department of Education
23 State House Station
Augusta, ME 04333-0023
207-624-6600
www.state.me.us/education/
Job link: www.state.me.us/education/
jobs.htm

Maryland

Maryland State Department of
Education
200 W. Baltimore St.
Baltimore, MD 21201
410-767-0600
www.marylandpublicschools.org/msde
Job link:
www.marylandpublicschools.org/
MSDE/aboutmsde/jobs/careers.htm

Massachusetts

Massachusetts Department of
Education
350 Main St.
Malden, MA 02148-5023
781-338-3000
www.doe.mass.edu
Job link: www.doe.mass.edu/jobs/

Michigan

Michigan Department of Education
608 W. Allegan Street
PO Box 30008
Lansing, MI 48909
517-373-3324
www.michigan.gov/mde
Job link:
www.michigan.gov/mde/0,1607,
7-140-6530_25538_6565---,00.html

Minnesota

Minnesota Department of Education
1500 Hwy. 36 W.
Roseville, MN 55113-4266
651-582-8200
http://education.state.mn.us/mde/
index.html
Job link: http://education.state.mn.us/
mde/About_MDE/Employment/
index.html

Mississippi

Mississippi Department of Education
Central High School Building
PO Box 771
359 N. West St.
Jackson, MS 39205
601-359-3513
www.mde.k12.ms.us
Job link: www.mde.k12.ms.us/
human_resources/emp_opps.html

Missouri

Missouri Department of Elementary
and Secondary Education
PO Box 480
Jefferson City, MO 65102
573-751-4212
www.dese.state.mo.us
Job link:
www.dese.state.mo.us/divadm/
humanres/vacancies.html

Montana

Montana Office of Public Instruction
PO Box 202501
Helena, MT 59620-2501
888-231-9393
www.opi.state.mt.us
Job link: www.opi.state.mt.us/
Index.html

Nebraska

Nebraska Department of Education
301 Centennial Mall S.
PO Box 94987
Lincoln, NE 68509
402-471-2295
www.nde.state.ne.us
Job link: www.nde.state.ne.us/HR/
page2.htm

Nevada
Nevada Department of Education
700 E. 5th St.
Carson City, NV 89701
775-687-9200
www.doe.nv.gov
Job link: www.doe.nv.gov/employ.html

New Hampshire
New Hampshire Department of
Education
101 Pleasant St.
Concord, NH 03301-3860
603-271-1953
www.ed.state.nh.us
Job link: www.ed.state.nh.us/
education/doe/employ.htm

New Jersey
New Jersey Department of Education
100 Riverview Plaza
PO Box 500
Trenton, NJ 08625-0500
609-292-4469
www.state.nj.us/education/
Job link: www.state.nj.us/njded/genfo/
vacancy.htm

New Mexico
New Mexico Public Education
Department
300 Don Gaspar
Santa Fe, NM 87501-2786
505-827-5800
www.sde.state.nm.us
Job link: www.nmreap.net/
indexJobs.htm

New York
New York State Education Department
89 Washington Ave.
Albany, NY 12234

www.nysed.gov
Job link: www.oms.nysed.gov/hr/

North Carolina
North Carolina Department of Public
Instruction
301 N. Wilmington St.
Raleigh, NC 27601
919-807-3300
www.dpi.state.nc.us
Job link: www.ncpublicschools.org/
employment.html

North Dakota
North Dakota Department of Public
Instruction
600 E. Boulevard Ave., Dept. 201
Bismarck, ND 58505-0440
701-328-2260
www.dpi.state.nd.us
Job link: www.dpi.state.nd.us/dept/
employ.shtm

Ohio
Ohio Department of Education
25 S. Front St.
Columbus, OH 43215-4183
877-644-6338
www.ode.state.oh.us
Job link: www.ode.state.oh.us/jobs.asp

Oklahoma
Oklahoma State Department of
Education
2500 N. Lincoln Blvd.
Oklahoma City, OK 73105-4599
405-521-3301
www.sde.state.ok.us/home/
defaultie.html

Oregon

Oregon Department of Education
255 Capitol St. NE
Salem, OR 97310-0203
503-378-3569
www.ode.state.or.us/
Job link: www.ode.state.or.us/search/
results/?id=71

Pennsylvania

Pennsylvania Department of
Education
333 Market St.
Harrisburg, PA 17126
717-783-6788
www.pde.state.pa.us/pde_internet/site/
default.asp
Job link: www.teaching.state.pa.us/
teaching/cwp/

Rhode Island

Rhode Island Department of
Education
255 Westminster St.
Providence, RI 02903
401-222-4600
www.ridoe.net

South Carolina

South Carolina Department of
Education
1429 Senate St.
Columbia, SC 29201
803-734-8500
www.sde.state.sc.us
Job link: www.carolinacareers.org

South Dakota

South Dakota Department of
Education
700 Governors Dr.
Pierre, SD 57501
605-773-3134
http://doe.sd.gov

Tennessee

Tennessee Department of Education
Andrew Johnson Tower, 6th Floor
Nashville, TN 37243-0375
615-741-2731
www.state.tn.us/education/
Job link:
https://www.k-12.state.tn.us/teachtn/

Texas

Texas Education Agency
1701 N. Congress Ave.
Austin, TX 78701
512-463-9734
www.tea.state.tx.us
Job link: www.tea.state.tx.us/hr/jvn/

Utah

Utah State Office of Education
250 E. 500 S.
PO Box 144200
Salt Lake City, UT 84114-4200
www.usoe.k12.ut.us
Job link: www.usoe.k12.ut.us/jobs/

Vermont

Vermont Department of Education
120 State St.
Montpelier, VT 05620-2501
www.state.vt.us/educ/
Job link: www.state.vt.us/educ/new/
html/mainemploy.html

Virginia

Virginia Department of Education
PO Box 2120
Richmond, VA 23218
800-292-3820
www.pen.k12.va.us
Job link: www.pen.k12.va.us/VDOE/
JOVE/home.shtml

Washington
Washington State Department of
Public Instruction
Old Capitol Building
PO Box 47200
Olympia, WA 98504-7200
360-725-6000
www.k12.wa.us

West Virginia
West Virginia Department of
Education
1900 Kanawha Blvd. E.
Charleston, WV 25305
800-982-2378
http://wvde.state.wv.us/
Job link: http://wvde.state.wv.us/jobs/

Wisconsin
Wisconsin Department of Public
Instruction
125 S. Webster St.
PO Box 7841
Madison, WI 53707-7841
800-441-4563
www.dpi.state.wi.us/
Job link: www.dpi.state.wi.us/jbsintro.html

Wyoming
Wyoming Department of Education
2300 Capitol Ave.
Hathaway Building, 2nd Floor
Cheyenne, WY 82002-0050
307-777-7690
www.k12.wy.us

State Offices of Teacher Certification

Web sites for state offices of teacher certification include links that offer updated requirements for certification and, in many cases, list job opportunities in the state.

Alabama
Alabama Department of Education
404 State Office Building
Montgomery, AL 36130-3901
205-261-5290
www.alsde.edu/html/sections/
section_detail.asp?section=
66&footer=sections

Alaska
Alaska Department of Education
Teacher Education and Certification
Attn: Assessment Center
801 W. 10th St., Ste. 200
Juneau, AK 99801-1894
907-465-2831
www.eed.state.ak.us

Arizona
Arizona Department of Education
Teacher Certification Unit
1535 W. Jefferson St.
Phoenix, AZ 85007
800-352-4558
602-542-5393
www.ade.state.az.us

Arkansas
Arkansas Department of Education
Teacher Education/Licensure
4 Capitol Mall
Little Rock, AR 72201
501-682-4475
http://arkedu.state.ar.us

California

California Commission on Teacher
Credentialing
1900 Capitol Ave.
Sacramento, CA 95814-4213
916-445-0184
www.ctc.ca.gov

Colorado

Colorado Department of Education,
Educator Licensing
State Office Building
201 E. Colfax Ave.
Denver, CO 80203-1799
303-866-6600
www.cde.state.co.us

Connecticut

Connecticut State Department of
Education
Bureau of Certification and Teacher
Preparation
PO Box 150471
Room 243
Hartford, CT 06115-0471
860-566-5201
www.state.ct.us/sde

Delaware

Delaware Department of Education
Licensure/Certification Office
401 Federal St., Ste. 2
Dover, DE 19901
888-759-9133
302-739-4686
http://deeds.doe.k12.de.us

District of Columbia

Division of Teacher Services
District of Columbia Public Schools
415 12th St. N.W.
Room 1013
Washington, DC 20004-1994
202-724-4250
www.k12.dc.us/dcps/home.html

Florida

Florida Department of Education
Bureau of Teacher Certification
Turlington Building
325 W. Gaines St.
Tallahassee, FL 32399
850-245-0505
www.firn.edu/doe

Georgia

Georgia Professional Standards
Commission
2 Peachtree St., Ste. 6000
Atlanta, GA 30303
800-869-7775
404-232-2500
www.gapsc.com

Hawaii

Hawaii Department of Education
Office of Personnel Services
Teacher Recruitment Unit
PO Box 2360
Honolulu, HI 96804
808-586-3420
http://doe.k12.hi.us

Idaho

Idaho Department of Education
Bureau of Certification and
Professional Standards
PO Box 83720
Boise, ID 83720-0027
800-432-4601
208-332-6800
www.sde.state.id.us/certification/

Illinois

Illinois State Board of Education
Division of Professional Preparation
100 N. First St.
Springfield, IL 62777
866-262-6663
www.isbe.state.il.us

Indiana

Indiana Department of Education
Division of Professional Standards
251 E. Ohio St., Ste. 201
Indianapolis, IN 46204
866-542-3672
317-232-9010
www.doe.state.in.us/dps/

Iowa

Iowa Board of Educational Examiners
Grimes State Office Building
Des Moines, IA 50319-0143
515-281-5294
www.state.ia.us//boee

Kansas

Kansas State Department of
Education
Division of Certification
120 SE 10th Ave.
Topeka, KS 66612
785-296-3204
www.ksbe.state.ks.us

Kentucky

Kentucky Department of Education
Office of Teacher
Education/Certification
1024 Capital Center Dr., Ste. 225
Frankfort, KY 40601
502-573-4606
www.kde.state.ky.us

Louisiana

Louisiana Department of Education
Division of Teacher Standards,
Assessment, and Certification
PO Box 44064
Baton Rouge, LA 70804-9064
225-342-3490
www.doe.state.la.us/lde/index.html

Maine

Maine Department of Education
Certification and Placement
23 State House Station
Augusta, ME 04333-0023
207-287-5944
www.state.me.us/education/

Maryland

Maryland State Department of
Education
Division of Certification and
Accreditation
200 W. Baltimore St.
Baltimore, MD 21201
410-767-0412
www.marylandpublicschools.org/msde

Massachusetts

Massachusetts Department of
Education
Teacher Certification Center
350 Main St.
Malden, MA 02148-5023
781-338-3000
www.doe.mass.edu

Michigan

Michigan Department of Education
Office of Professional Preparation and
Certification Services
PO Box 30008
Lansing, MI 48909
517-373-3324
www.michigan.gov/mde

Minnesota

Minnesota Department of Children,
Families, and Learning Teacher
Licensing
1500 Hwy. 36 W.
Roseville, MN 55113-4266
651-582-8200
www.education.state.mn.us/mde

Mississippi

Mississippi Department of Education,
Teacher Center
PO Box 771
Jackson, MS 39205-0771
601-359-3513
www.mde.k12.ms.us

Missouri

Missouri Department of Elementary
and Secondary Education
Division of Urban and Teacher
Education
Teacher Certification
PO Box 480
Jefferson City, MO 65102
573-751-4212
www.dese.state.mo.us

Montana

Montana Office of Public Instruction
Teacher Education/Certification
PO Box 202501
Helena, MT 59620-2501
888-231-9393
406-444-3095
www.opi.state.mt.us

Nebraska

Nebraska Department of Education
Teacher Certification
301 Centennial Mall S.
PO Box 94987
Lincoln, NE 68509
402-471-2295
www.nde.state.ne.us

Nevada

Nevada Department of Education
Teacher Licensure
1820 E. Sahara Ave., Ste. 205
Las Vegas, NV 89104
702-486-6458
www.doe.nv.gov

New Hampshire

New Hampshire Department of
Education
Bureau of Credentialing
101 Pleasant St.
Concord, NH 03301-3860
603-271-3494
www.ed.state.nh.us

New Jersey

New Jersey Department of Education
Office of Licensing and Credentials
100 Riverview Plaza
PO Box 500
Trenton, NJ 08625-0500
609-292-4469
www.state.nj.us/education

New Mexico

New Mexico Public Education
Department
Professional Licensure Unit
300 Don Gaspar
Santa Fe, NM 87501-2786
505-827-5800
http://sde.state.nm.us

New York

New York State Education
Department
Office of Teaching
89 Washington Avenue
Albany, NY 12234
518-474-3852
www.nysed.gov

North Carolina

North Carolina Department of Public
Instruction
Licensure Section
301 N. Wilmington St.
Raleigh, NC 27601-2825
919-733-0377
www.dpi.state.nc.us

North Dakota

North Dakota Educational Standards
and Practices Board
Teacher Licensure Office
600 E. Boulevard Ave.
Bismarck, ND 58505-0440
701-328-2260
www.dpi.state.nd.us

Ohio

Ohio Department of Education
Certification and Licensure
25 S. Front St.
Columbus, OH 43215-4183
877-644-6338 or 614-466-2761
www.ode.state.oh.us

Oklahoma

Oklahoma State Department of
Education
Professional Standards Section
Teacher Certification
2500 N. Lincoln Blvd.
Oklahoma City, OK 73105-4599
405-521-6205
http://sde.state.ok.us

Oregon

Oregon Teacher Standards and
Practices Commission
465 Commercial St. NE
Salem, OR 97301
503-378-3586
www.tspc.state.or.us

Pennsylvania

Pennsylvania Department of
Education
Bureau of Teacher Certification and
Preparation
333 Market St.
Harrisburg, PA 17126
717-783-6788
www.pde.psu.edu

Rhode Island

Rhode Island Department of
Elementary and Secondary Education
Office of Teacher Preparation
Certification and Professional
Development
255 Westminster St.
Providence, RI 02903
401-222-4600
www.ridoe.net
Job link: www.ridoe.net/teachers/
ed_employment.htm

South Carolina
South Carolina Department of
Education
Teacher Education/Certification
Landmark II Office Building
3700 Forest Dr., Ste. 500
Columbia, SC 29204
877-885-5280
803-734-8466
www.scteachers.org

South Dakota
South Dakota Department of
Education and Cultural Affairs
Office Policy and Account
Certification
Kniep Building, 3rd Floor
700 Governors Dr.
Pierre, SD 57501
605-773-3134
http://doe.sd.gov

Tennessee
Tennessee Department of Education
Office of Teacher Licensing
Andrew Johnson Tower
6th Floor
Nashville, TN 37243-0375
615-741-2731
www.state.tn.us/education

Texas
Texas State Board for Educator
Certification
1701 N. Congress Ave.
WBT 5-100
Austin, TX 78701-1494
888-863-5880
512-936-8400
www.sbec.state.tx.us

Utah
Utah State Office of Education
Educator Licensing
250 E. 500 S.
PO Box 144200
Salt Lake City, UT 84114-4200
801-538-7753
www.usoe.k12.ut.us

Vermont
Vermont Department of Education
Teacher Certification
120 State St.
Montpelier, VT 05620-2501
802-828-0584
www.state.vt.us/educ

Virginia
Virginia Department of Education
Division of Teacher Education and
Licensure
PO Box 2120
Richmond, VA 23218
800-292-3820
www.pen.k12.va.us

Washington
Washington Office of the
Superintendent of Public Instruction
Professional Certification
Old Capitol Building
PO Box 47200
Olympia, WA 98504-7200
360-725-6000
www.k12.wa.us

West Virginia
West Virginia Department of
Education
Teacher Certification
1900 Kanawha Blvd. E.
Charleston, WV 25305
800-982-2378
http://wvde.state.wv.us

Wisconsin
Wisconsin Department of Public
Instruction
Teacher Education and Licensing
PO Box 7841
Madison, WI 53707-7841
800-441-4563
608-266-3390
www.dpi.state.wi.us

Wyoming
Wyoming Professional Teaching
Standards Board
2300 Capitol Ave.
Hathaway Building, 2nd Floor
Cheyenne, WY 82002-0050
307-777-7690
www.k12.wy.us

NEA State Affiliates

The National Education Association (NEA) is the leading organization in the
United States for the advancement of public education. Each state's NEA affiliate Web site offers valuable information including educational news and links to
employment opportunities within each state.

Alabama Education Association
422 Dexter Ave.
PO Box 4177
Montgomery, AL 36103-4177
800-392-5839
334-834-9790
www.myaea.org

NEA–Alaska
114 2nd St.
Juneau, AK 99801
907-586-3090
www.ak.nea.org

Arizona Education Association
4000 N. Central Ave., Ste. 1600
Phoenix, AZ 85012
800-352-5411
602-264-1774
www.arizonaea.org

Arkansas Education Association
1500 W. 4th St.
Little Rock, AR 72201
800-632-0624
501-375-4611
www.aeaonline.org

California Teachers Association
1705 Murchison Dr.
PO Box 921
Burlingame, CA 94011-0921
650-697-1400
www.cta.org

Colorado Education Association
1500 Grant St.
Denver, CO 80203-1800
800-332-5939
303-837-1500
www.coloradoea.org

Connecticut Education Association
Capitol Place, Ste. 500
21 Oak St.
Hartford, CT 06106-8001
800-842-4316
860-525-5641
www.cea.org

Delaware State Education Association
136 E. Water St.
Dover, DE 19901
800-736-3732
302-734-5834

Florida Education Association
213 S. Adams St.
Tallahassee, FL 32301
850-201-2800
www.floridaea.org

Georgia Association of Educators
100 Crescent Center Pkwy., Ste. 500
Tucker, GA 30084
800-282-7142
678-837-1100
www.gae.org

Hawaii State Teachers Association
1200 Ala Kapuna St.
Honolulu, HI 96819
800-352-3504
808-833-2711
www.hsta.org

Idaho Education Association
PO Box 2638
Boise, ID 83701
208-344-1341
www.idahoea.org

Illinois Education Association–NEA
100 E. Edwards St.
Springfield, IL 62704-1999
217-544-0706
www.ieanea.org

Indiana State Teachers Association
150 W. Market St., Ste. 900
Indianapolis, IN 46204-2875
800-382-4037
317-263-3400
www.ista-in.org

Iowa State Education Association
777 3rd St.
Des Moines, IA 50309
800-445-9358
515-471-8000
www.isea.org

Kansas NEA
715 SW 10th Ave.
Topeka, KS 66612-1686
785-232-8271
www.knea.org

Kentucky Education Association
401 Capitol Ave.
Frankfort, KY 40601
800-231-4532
502-227-8062
www.kea.org

Louisiana Association of Educators
PO Box 479
Baton Rouge, LA 70821
877-452-3477
225-343-9243
www.lae.org

Maine Education Association
35 Community Dr.
Augusta, ME 04330
800-452-8709
207-622-5866
www.maine.nea.org

Maryland State Teachers Association
140 Main St.
Annapolis, MD 21401
800-448-6782
410-263-6600
www.mstanea.org

Massachusetts Teachers Association
20 Ashburton Pl.
Boston, MA 02108
800-392-6175
617-878-8000
617-742-7950
www.massteacher.org

Michigan Education Association
1216 Kendale Blvd.
PO Box 2573
East Lansing, MI 48826-2573
800-292-1934
517-332-6551
www.mea.org

Education Minnesota
41 Sherburne Ave.
St. Paul, MN 55103
800-652-9073
651-227-9541
www.educationminnesota.org

Mississippi Association of Educators
775 N. State St.
Jackson, MS 39202
800-530-7998
601-354-4463
www.ms.nea.org

Missouri–NEA
1810 E. Elm St.
Jefferson City, MO 65101
573-634-3202
www.mnea.org

Montana Education Association
1232 E. 6th Ave.
Helena, MT 59601
800-398-0826
406-442-4250
www.mea-mft.org

Nebraska State Education Association
605 S. 14th
Lincoln, NE 68508
402-475-7611
www.nsea.org

Nevada State Education Association
1890 Donald St.
Reno, NV 89502
800-232-6732
775-828-6732

3511 E. Harmon Ave.
Las Vegas, NV 89121
800-248-6732
702-733-7330
www.nsea-nv.org

NEA–New Hampshire
103 N. State St.
Concord, NH 03301
603-224-7751
www.neanh.org

New Jersey Education Association
180 W. State St.
PO Box 1211
Trenton, NJ 08607-1211
609-599-4561
www.njea.org

NEA–New Mexico
PO Box 729
Santa Fe, NM 87501-0729
505-982-1916
www.nea-nm.org

NEA–New York
217 Lark St.
Albany, NY 12210
800-666-3269
518-462-6451
www.neany.org

North Carolina Association of Educators
700 S. Salisbury St.
Raleigh, NC 27601
800-662-7924
www.ncae.org

North Dakota Education Association
410 E. Thayer Ave.
Bismarck, ND 58501
800-369-6332
701-223-0450
www.ndea.org

Ohio Education Association
225 E. Broad St.
Columbus, OH 43216
614-228-4526
www.ohea.org

Oklahoma Education Association
323 E. Madison
Oklahoma City, OK 73105
800-522-8091
405-528-7785
www.okea.org

Oregon Education Association
6900 SW Atlanta St.
Portland, OR 97223
800-858-5505
503-684-3300
www.oregoned.org

Pennsylvania State Education Association
400 N. 3rd St.
PO Box 1724
Harrisburg, PA 17105-1724
800-944-7732
717-255-7000
www.psea.org

NEA–Rhode Island
99 Bald Hill Rd.
Cranston, RI 02920
401-463-9630
www.neari.org

South Carolina Education Association
421 Zimalcrest Dr.
Columbia, SC 29210
800-422-7232
803-772-6553
www.thescea.org

South Dakota Education Association
411 E. Capitol Ave.
Pierre, SD 57501
800-529-0090
605-224-9263
www.sdea.org

Tennessee Education Association
801 Second Ave. N.
Nashville, TN 37201-1099
800-342-8367
615-242-8392
www.teateachers.org

Texas State Teachers Association
316 W. 12th St.
Austin, TX 78701
877-275-8782
www.tsta.org

Utah Education Association
875 E. 5180 S.
Murray, UT 84107-5299
800-594-8996
801-266-4461
www.utea.org

Vermont–NEA
10 Wheelock St.
Montpelier, VT 05602-3737
802-223-6375
www.vtnea.org

Virginia Education Association
116 S. 3rd St.
Richmond, VA 23219
804-648-5801
www.veaweteach.org

Washington Education Association
PO Box 9100
Federal Way, WA 98063-9100
800-622-3393
253-941-6700
www.wa.nea.org

West Virginia Education Association
1558 Quarrier St.
Charleston, WV 25311
800-642-8261
304-346-5315
www.wvea.org

Wisconsin Education Association Council
33 Nob Hill Dr.
PO Box 8003
Madison, WI 53708-8003
608-276-7711
www.weac.org

Wyoming Education Association
115 E. 22nd St., Ste. 1
Cheyenne, WY 82001-3795
800-442-2395
www.wyoea.org

Federal Education Association
1201 16th St. NW, Ste. 117
Washington, DC 20036
202-822-7850
www.feaonline.org

Opportunities for Overseas Employment

This section lists some of the most important resources for information on teaching opportunities overseas.

Department of Defense Education Activity
4040 N. Fairfax Dr.
Arlington, VA 22203-1634
703-588-3983
www.dodea.edu

Fulbright Teacher Exchange Program
600 Maryland Ave. SW, Ste. 320
Washington, DC 20024
202-314-3527
www.fulbrightexchanges.org

Institute of International Education
809 United Nations Plaza
New York, NY 10017
212-883-8200
www.iie.org

International Schools Services
15 Roszel Rd.
PO Box 5910
Princeton, NJ 08543
609-452-0990
www.iss.edu

Peace Corps
1111 20th St. NW
Washington, DC 20526
800-424-8580
www.peacecorps.gov

U.S. Department of State
Office of Overseas Schools
2201 C St. NW
Washington, DC 20520
202-647-6575
www.state.gov/m/a/os/

U.S. Territories

Each U.S. territory has teaching opportunities. Contact information is included for each territory, including Web sites that tell about schools, programs, and employment opportunities, as well as recent press releases. The amount of helpful information varies with each site. You might need to call to get the specific information you need.

American Samoa Department of Education
Pago Pago, American Samoa 96799
684-633-5237
www.doe.as

Commonwealth of Puerto Rico
Department of Education
PO Box 190759
San Juan, PR 00919-0759
787-754-8926

Commonwealth of the Northern Mariana Islands
Public School System
PO Box 501370
Saipan, MP 96950
670-664-3721
www.cnmi.net/community.php

Guam Public School System
PO Box DE
Agana, Guam 96932
671-475-0495
www.doe.edu.gu

Virgin Islands Department of Education
44-46 Kongens Gade
Charlotte Amalie, VI 00802
340-774-0100
www.usvi.org/education/

Additional Overseas Employment Resources

This section offers five important resources for information on overseas employment opportunities.

Overseas Employment Information for Teachers
Department of State
Washington, DC 20520
www.usajobs.opm.gov/ei26.asp

TESOL: Teachers of English to Speakers of Other Languages
700 S. Washington St., Ste. 200
Alexandria, VA 22314
888-547-3369
703-836-0774
www.tesol.org/careers/

TIE: The International Educator
PO Box 513
Cummaquid, MA 02637
877-375-6668
508-362-1414
www.tieonline.com

UNI Overseas Placement Service for Educators
University of Northern Iowa Advising and Career Services
242 Gilchrist Hall
Cedar Falls, IA 50614-0390
319-273-2083
www.uni.edu/placement/overseas/

Index

D

E